COUNTRY HOUSES
OF SWEDEN

LANDHÄUSER
IN SCHWEDEN

LES MAISONS
ROMANTIQUES
DE SUÈDE

COUNTRY HOUSES OF SWEDEN

LANDHÄUSER IN SCHWEDEN

LES MAISONS ROMANTIQUES DE SUÈDE

Barbara & René Stoeltie

EDITED BY · HERAUSGEGEBEN VON · SOUS LA DIRECTION DE

Angelika Taschen

TASCHEN

KÖLN LONDON MADRID NEW YORK PARIS TOKYO

CONTENTS
INHALT
SOMMAIRE

ROMANTIC COUNTRY HOUSES OF *S*WEDEN

Carl Larsson, *Catching Crayfish · Krebsfang · La pêche au crabe* (1890–1899), detail, Nationalmuseum, Stockholm

ABOVE · OBEN · CI-DESSUS: Carl Larsson, *The Flower Window · Das Blumenfester · La fenêtre fleurie* (1890–1899), detail, Nationalmuseum, Stockholm

Sweden is a country of islands, lakes and forests. It is also the land of the midnight sun and the northern lights, where to our surprise there are still pastures stretching to the horizon, and yellow and red country houses which seem to actively refuse all other colours. Sweden is a place of architectural beauty, dotted with magnificent castles, manors and "herrgårdors" with names like Haga, Skogaholm, and Skokloster. All these evoke the past and the memory of kings and great lords. In such places, enormous rooms with pale floorboards and walls covered with family portraits serve as a backdrop to elegant, pastel-toned tables, chairs and sideboards. This quintessentially Swedish furniture borrowed its original outlines from France; corrected and revised by Gustavus III, the great king-arbiter of good taste, it carries the beautiful name of "gustaviansk", Gustavian.

Sweden is the chosen country of painters, writers, musicians and architects. Tessin, Alexander Roslin, Johan Tobias Sergel, Olof Tempelman, the Masreliez family, Louis Jean Desprez, Carl Hårleman, Fredrik Magnus Piper, Georg Haupt and Erik Öhrmark all worked there. On the skins of his golden-haired bathers, the painter Anders Zorn captured the peculiar quality of sunshine in his native land, as well as its flickering reflection. Selma Lagerlöf, the writer, invented

ROMANTISCHE LANDHÄUSER IN *S*CHWEDEN

Carl Larsson, *The Yard and the Washhouse · Der Hof und das Waschhaus · La ferme et la buanderie* (1890–1899), Nationalmuseum, Stockholm

Schweden besteht aus zahllosen Inseln und Inselchen. Schweden, übersät von Seen und Wäldern, ist das Land der Mitternachtssonne und des Nordlichts, das den Blick überrascht mit horizontweiten Weidegründen und mit Landhäusern so rot oder gelb, als wollten sie keine andere Farbe annehmen. Ein Gefilde von Schönheiten, geschmückt mit prächtigen Schlössern, mit Gütern und »herrgårdor«, in deren Namen – Haga, Skogaholm, Skokloster – die Vergangenheit fortlebt und die Erinnerung an Könige und Gutsherren wach wird. Hier, in den weitläufigen Salons mit hellen Holzböden und von Familienportraits bedeckten Wänden, stehen elegante Möbel in Pastelltönen, deren Formen einst aus Frankreich kamen und, nachdem sie von Gustav III. mit sicherem Geschmack geprüft und anverwandelt worden waren, den hübschen Namen »gustaviansk« erhielten. Zahlreiche Maler, Schriftsteller, Musiker und Architekten haben in Schweden ihre Wahlheimat gefunden. Die Tessins, Alexander Roslin, Johan Tobias Sergel, Olof Tempelman, die Masreliez-Familie, Louis Jean Desprez, Carl Hårleman, Fredrik Magnus Piper, Georg Haupt und Erik Öhrmark haben hier ihrem Traum Gestalt verliehen. Hier fing der Maler Anders Zorn mit feinem Pinsel das Sonnenlicht ein und ließ es zart auf der Haut seiner blonden Badenden schimmern, und hier erzählte Selma Lagerlöf die außerordentliche Geschichte von Nils Holgersson, jenem unerschrockenen klei-

Carl Larsson, *The Kitchen · Die Küche · La cuisine* (1890–1899), Nationalmuseum, Stockholm

LES MAISONS ROMANTIQUES DE *S*UÈDE

La Suède … composée d'innombrables îles et îlots et parsemée de lacs et de forêts. La Suède … pays du soleil de minuit et de l'aurore boréale, où le regard surpris découvre des pâturages qui s'étendent jusqu'à l'horizon et des maisons de campagne, rouges ou jaunes, qui semblent refuser tout autre couleur. Terre de beauté, parée de châteaux, de manoirs et de «herrgårdor» magnifiques dont les noms – Haga, Skogaholm, Skokloster – évoquent le passé et le souvenir des rois et des grands seigneurs. Leurs vastes salons aux planchers blonds et aux murs couverts de portraits de famille servent de décor à un mobilier aux tons pastel qui emprunta jadis ses formes élégantes à la France et qui – revu et corrigé par l'arbitre du bon goût qui s'appelait Gustave III – s'enrichit du beau nom de «gustaviansk».

La Suède est la terre d'élection de peintres, d'écrivains, de musiciens et d'architectes. Les Tessin, Alexander Roslin, Johan Tobias Sergel, Olof Tempelman, la famille Masreliez, Louis Jean Desprez, Carl Hårleman, Fredrik Magnus Piper, Georg Haupt et Erik Öhrmark y ont réalisé leur rêve en trois dimensions. Le peintre Anders Zorn captait ici les rayons de soleil du bout de son pinceau et les faisait miroiter délicatement sur la peau de ses baigneuses blondes; Selma Lagerlöf nous a raconté l'histoire extraordinaire de Nils Holgersson, le petit garçon courageux qui survola son pays sur le dos d'une oie, afin d'en découvrir les multiples merveilles.

Carl Larsson, *Apple Blossom · Apfelblüte · Fleurs de pommier* (1894), detail, private collection · Privatbesitz · collection particulière

the wonderful tale of Nils Holgersson, the courageous boy who flew over the land on the back of a goose, discovering wonder after wonder along the way.

Sweden was also the birthplace of the great naturalist Carl von Linné (Linnaeus), the first scholar to describe vast numbers of plant species; also of the illustrator Carl Larsson, who, inspired by a mixture of deep affection and a desire to pay homage to life in the countryside, immortalised his family and his house at Sundborn. More recently, Sweden has produced the character of Pippi Longstocking, the *enfant terrible* created by Astrid Lindgren, ever young and ever ready to challenge accepted values.

The traditional cooking in Sweden is extremely tasty: a "smörgåsbord" of fresh prawns washed down with a shot of ice-cold "aquavit" is not to be spurned, any more than a fried fresh herring sprinkled with dill, or marinated salmon accompanied by a sweet-and-sour sauce. These are only some of the many excellent reasons for visiting the Scandinavian north, or for sailing out to one of the thousands of islands that make up its Baltic archipelago. Here we may come upon a perfect fisherman's cottage, perhaps even an abandoned artist's studio built on the rocks fronting the Baltic Sea. If we're lucky, we may even find ourselves relaxing on a wooden bench in some venerable farmhouse, warming our feet by a cavernous whitewashed fireplace.

Sweden has all this – and more. It is a country which will never cease to intrigue us, and to whose people we will always feel able to say, as the Swedes themselves say to each other: I love you, I salute you.

nen Jungen, der auf dem Rücken eines Gänserichs flog, um die zahlreichen Wunder seiner Heimat zu entdecken.

In Schweden geboren wurde jedoch auch der Naturforscher Carl von Linné, der so viele Pflanzenarten beschrieb. Ebenso der Illustrator Carl Larsson, der aus inniger Hingabe wie aus dem tief empfundenen Wunsch, das Landleben zu loben, der Nachwelt ein vielfältiges und bemerkenswert akribisches Bild von seiner Familie und seinem Haus in Sundborn hinterließ. Und vor gar nicht so langer Zeit ersann hier Astrid Lindgren die ewig junge Göre Pippi Langstrumpf, die nur darauf wartet, mit allen Konventionen zu brechen.

Viele von uns lernen auch die kulinarischen Traditionen Schwedens schätzen – ob nun das reichhaltige »smörgåsbord« mit Krabben nebst einem Glas eiskalten Aquavit, den mit Aniskraut bestreuten gebratenen Hering oder den marinierten Salm in einer sämigen, süßsauren Sauce. Es gibt also gute Gründe, sich in den Norden aufzumachen und eines der Tausenden Inselchen des Archipels anzusteuern. Man wird dort auf die eine oder andere Fischerhütte stoßen, vielleicht sogar auf ein in die Felsen gebautes verlassenes Künstleratelier mit Blick auf die Ostsee. Man wird in einem alten Bauernhof Rast machen, wo es wohl tut, auf einer langen Bank auszuruhen und sich am großen gekälkten Kamin zu wärmen, in dem ein einladendes Holzfeuer knistert.

Alles dies ist Schweden. Ein Land, das uns immer faszinieren wird und zu dem wir sagen können: Sei mir gegrüßt, ich hab dich gern.

Carl Larsson, *Lisbeth Fishing · Lisbeth angelt · Lisbeth à la pêche* (1900), detail, Nationalmuseum, Stockholm

La Suède, c'est aussi la terre natale du naturaliste Carl von Linné qui décrivit tant d'espèces végétales, de l'illustrateur Carl Larsson qui immortalisa sa famille et sa maison de Sundborn avec une minutie remarquable, inspirée à la fois par l'affection et par le désir profond de rendre hommage à la vie campagnarde. Plus récemment, elle a vu naître Fifi Brindacier, l'enfant terrible imaginée par une Astrid Lindgren, toujours jeune et prête à bousculer les valeurs sûres.

Nous sommes également nombreux à découvrir avec plaisir en Suède des traditions culinaires à l'image du pays, qu'il s'agisse du «smörgåsbord» somptueux aux crevettes grises accompagné d'un verre d'aquavit glacé, du hareng poêlé saupoudré d'aneth ou du saumon mariné accompagné d'une sauce aigredouce onctueuse. Voilà de bien bonnes raisons de visiter les contrées nordiques et de s'embarquer pour une des milliers d'îles qui composent l'archipel. Nous y découvrirons quelque gîte de pêcheur, peut-être même un atelier d'artiste abandonné bâti sur les rochers face à la mer Baltique; nous nous attarderons dans une vieille ferme où il fait bon se reposer sur une longue banquette et se réchauffer à côté d'une vaste hotte blanchie à la chaux où crépite un feu de bois accueillant.

La Suède, c'est tout cela. Un pays qui ne cessera jamais de nous fasciner et auquel nous pouvons dire: je vous salue et je vous aime.

Carl Larsson, *The Hut · Die Hütte · La cabane* (1890–1899), Nationalmuseum, Stockholm

$\mathcal{K}$ARIN OCH CARL LARSSON

Dalarna

In his celebrated book *Ett hem,* the illustrator Carl Larsson (1853–1919) describes how he discovered his house in Dalecarlia on making a detour by way of Sundborn, where his father-in-law's two sisters were living on a small farm called Lilla Hyttnäs. On the spot, Larsson decided to leave the noisy city and move into an environment where the beauty of nature was all around him. In a letter written to his wife Karin in 1903, he describes the first moments he spent at Lilla Hyttnäs: "Do you know, those first minutes I spent in our little house were so delicious: I lit all the lamps, inspected every corner and opened all the doors. I truly believe that we have created something beautiful." The Larssons did indeed make their house into a work of art, and their day-to-day existence was no different. Everything around them – furniture, objects, colours – became special. The thousands who visit their "world" today and recognise each detail that Carl so painstakingly illustrated, can readily identify the motto placed over the door: "Welcome, friend, to the house of Carl Larsson and his wife".

In seinem berühmten Buch »Ett hem« beschreibt der Illustrator Carl Larsson (1853–1919), wie er sein Haus in der Provinz Dalarna fand, als er einen Umweg über Sundborn machte, wo die beiden Schwestern seines Schwiegervaters auf einem kleinen Bauernhof namens Lilla Hyttnäs wohnten. Larsson verspürte daraufhin das Bedürfnis, die lärmende Stadt zu verlassen und sich in einer Umgebung anzusiedeln, in der die Schönheit der Natur den Ton angab. In einem Brief, den er 1903 an seine Frau Karin schrieb, erinnert er sich an die ersten Augenblicke in Lilla Hyttnäs: »Weißt du, diese ersten Momente in unserem kleinen Haus waren so köstlich: Ich zündete alle Lampen an, besichtigte jeden Winkel und öffnete alle Türen, und ich finde wahrhaftig, dass wir etwas sehr Schönes daraus geschaffen haben.« Tatsächlich haben die Larssons aus ihrem Haus ein regelrechtes Kunstwerk gemacht, dem auch ihr Alltag entsprach. Alles, was die Larssons anfassten, ob Möbel, Objekte oder Farben, wurde zu etwas Außergewöhnlichem, und die Tausenden, die heute ihre »Welt« besichtigen und jede von Larsson illustrierte Einzelheit wiedererkennen, begreifen mit einem Mal, was die Devise bedeutet, die das einzigartige Künstlerpaar über der Eingangstür aufgemalt hat: »Sei willkommen, lieber Freund, bei Carl Larsson und seiner Frau«.

Dans son célèbre livre «Ett hem», l'illustrateur Carl Larsson (1853–1919) décrit comment il a découvert sa maison en Dalécarlie, en faisant un détour par Sundborn où les deux sœurs de son beau-père vivaient dans une petite ferme nommée Lilla Hyttnäs. Larsson éprouva alors le besoin de quitter la ville bruyante et de s'installer dans un environnement dominé par la beauté de la nature. Dans une lettre de 1903 à son épouse Karin, il évoque les premiers moments passés à Lilla Hyttnäs: «Sais-tu, ces premiers moments passés dans notre petite maison étaient si délicieux: j'allumais toutes les lampes, j'inspectais chaque coin et j'ouvrais toutes les portes et je crois vraiment que nous en avons fait quelque chose de beau …» Il est vrai que les Larsson avaient fait une véritable œuvre d'art de leur maison, et leur vie quotidienne suivait le pas. Tout ce que touchaient les Larsson, qu'il s'agisse d'un meuble, d'un objet, ou d'une couleur, devenait exceptionnel et les milliers de personnes qui visitent leur «monde» aujourd'hui et reconnaissent chaque détail illustré par Carl, comprennent soudain ce que signifie la devise peinte par ce couple d'artistes unique au-dessus de la porte d'entrée: «Bienvenue cher ami dans la maison de Carl Larsson et son épouse».

LEFT: In the "verkstaden" – the first studio built in 1890 adjoining Lilla Hyttnäs – a portrait of Karin decorates the doorway. Larsson wrote: "I have just painted my idol on the sliding door."

FACING PAGE: For the Larssons, the dining room was the main meeting point of the house, where the family gathered under the lamps with their red shades. The latter were designed by Larsson himself in imitation of cactus flowers.

LINKS: In der »verkstaden«, dem 1890 als Anbau zu Lilla Hyttnäs errichteten ersten Atelier, schmückt das Portrait Karins die Eingangstür. Larsson schrieb: »Soeben habe ich mein Idol auf die Schiebetür gemalt!«

RECHTE SEITE: Das Esszimmer war für die Larssons der wichtigste Treffpunkt im Haus. Dort versammelten sie sich unter den Lampen mit roten Schirmen, die Carl – von der Form einer Kaktusblüte inspiriert – entworfen hat.

A GAUCHE: Dans le «verkstaden» – le premier atelier construit en 1890 et annexé à Lilla Hyttnäs –, le portrait de Karin décore la porte d'entrée. Larsson écrit: «Je viens de peindre mon idole sur la porte coulissante …!»

PAGE DE DROITE: La salle à manger était pour les Larsson un véritable lieu de rencontre et on se réunissait sous les lampes à abatjour rouge – une idée de Carl –, inspirées par la forme d'une fleur de cactus.

RIGHT: The décor of the dining room was completed in 1890. The Larssons intended its bright colours to provide a vivid contrast to the silvery snow and the dark green of the surrounding pine forest.

FOLLOWING PAGES: The drawing room at Lilla Hyttnäs. Larsson called it "The Temple of Idleness" and immortalised it in numerous drawings.

RECHTS: Die Einrichtung des Esszimmers war 1890 fertiggestellt. Das Paar war überzeugt, dass die kräftigen Farben zum Dunkelgrün der Wälder und zum silbrigen Schnee einen lebhaften Kontrast bilden würden.

FOLGENDE DOPPELSEITE: Das Wohnzimmer von Lilla Hyttnäs. Larsson hatte es »Tempel der Faulheit« getauft und hat es in zahlreichen Zeichnungen verewigt.

A DROITE: La décoration de la salle à manger fut achevée en 1890. Le couple était convaincu que les couleurs franches formeraient un contraste vif avec le vert foncé des forêts de pin et la neige blafarde.

DOUBLE PAGE SUIVANTE: Le séjour de Lilla Hyttnäs. Larsson l'avait baptisé «Le Temple de la Paresse» et l'a immortalisé dans un grand nombre de dessins.

ABOVE: *Carl Larsson painted Brita's portrait on the door between the drawing room and the dining room. "Bellman" chairs are lined up along the walls.*

RIGHT: *An 18th-century tiled stove occupies one corner of the drawing room.*

FACING PAGE: *While the general atmosphere is relaxed, the positioning of the furniture shows that Larsson leaned towards formality – or rather, orderliness.*

OBEN: *Auf die Tür zwischen Wohn- und Esszimmer malte Larsson ein Portrait seiner Tochter Brita. An der Wand stehen »Bellman«-Stühle.*

RECHTS: *Der Kachelofen aus dem 18. Jahrhundert beherrscht die Ecke des Wohnzimmers.*

RECHTE SEITE: *Dem lockeren Ambiente zum Trotz lässt die Aufstellung der Möbel auf eine gewisse Förmlichkeit und Ordnungsliebe schließen.*

CI-DESSUS: *Dans le séjour, Larsson a peint le portrait de Brita sur la porte de la salle à manger. Les chaises «bellman» sont alignées le long des murs.*

A DROITE: *Le poêle en faïence 18ᵉ domine le coin du séjour.*

PAGE DE DROITE: *Si l'ambiance est décontractée, la position des meubles indique une tendance un rien formaliste et le goût de l'ordre.*

FACING PAGE: *The décor of the Larssons' guest bedroom – odd, but harmonious. Among many others, Prince Eugene and Selma Lagerlöf spent restful nights here.*
ABOVE: *Karin's loom and sewing machine, in the first studio: after 1899, the children used this space as a reading room and play room.*
RIGHT: *On New Year's Eve 1899, Larsson threw a big party to inaugurate his brand new studio. His bust still presides over his painting things and his pictures.*

LINKE SEITE: *Das Gästezimmer hatten die Larssons im alten Stil ausgestattet. Prinz Eugen und die Schriftstellerin Selma Lagerlöf haben hier erholsame Nächte verbracht.*
OBEN: *Karin stellte ihren Webstuhl und ihre Nähmaschine im ersten Atelier auf; nach 1899 versammelten sich dort die Kinder zum Spielen.*
RECHTS: *An Silvester 1899 gab Larsson einen großen Empfang zur Einweihung seines neuen Ateliers. Noch immer thront seine Büste inmitten seiner Gerätschaften und Werke.*

PAGE DE GAUCHE: *Dans la chambre d'amis, les Larsson avaient créé un décor à l'ancienne. Le Prince Eugène et l'écrivain Selma Lagerlöf y passèrent des nuits paisibles.*
CI-DESSUS: *Karin installa son métier à tisser et sa machine à coudre dans le premier atelier; après 1899, les enfants s'y réunissaient pour lire et jouer.*
A DROITE: *En 1899, à la veille du Nouvel An, Larsson inaugura son nouvel atelier. Son buste trône toujours au milieu de ses ustensiles et de ses œuvres.*

LEFT: *In the "verk-staden", the red pillar incorporated into the bench was used as a receptacle for the artist's watercolours.*
FACING PAGE: *Today, great care is still taken that the bouquets of flowers should harmonise with the spirit of the Larsson family. They are invariably very simple.*

LINKS: *Der rote Pfosten, der zur Sitzbank gehört, diente in der »verkstaden« einst zur Aufbewahrung der Farben des Künstlers.*
RECHTE SEITE: *Heute legt man großen Wert darauf, dass die Blumensträuße mit dem Geist der Larssons harmonieren – die Arrangements sind stets von mustergültiger Schlichtheit.*

A GAUCHE: *Dans le «verkstaden», le pilier rouge qui fait partie de la banquette servait jadis à ranger les couleurs de l'artiste.*
PAGE DE DROITE: *On veille à ce que les bouquets de fleurs restent en harmonie avec l'esprit des Larsson et les arrangements floraux sont toujours d'une simplicité exemplaire.*

Carl decorated his wife's bedroom with a frieze of stylised flower garlands and ribbons. Karin wove the curtain which separated their two chambers: the title of this remarkable piece was "The Rose of Love".

Carl dekorierte die Wände im Zimmer seiner Frau mit einem Fries aus Blumengirlanden und stilisierten Bändern. Karin webte den Vorhang, der die beiden Zimmer voneinander trennte. Sie nannte ihre bemerkenswerte Arbeit »die Liebesrose«.

Carl décora les murs de la chambre de sa femme avec une frise composée de guirlandes de fleurs et de rubans stylisés. Karin tissa le rideau qui séparait leurs deux chambres. Elle a baptisé son œuvre remarquable «La Rose de l'Amour».

ZORNGÅRDEN
Anders Zorn

Dalarna

The house of the painter Anders Zorn (1860–1920) is now a museum, but the spirit of its former occupant is still so overwhelmingly present that at any moment you half expect his large figure to fill the doorway. Zorn was the offspring of a passionate affair between a young Swedish girl and a German brewer, and he showed promise as a draftsman at a very early age. He attended the Fine Arts school in Stockholm and thereafter his success was meteoric. Today you need only look at his red-suited self-portrait, with its leonine head and imperious glance, to realise that Zorn must have been a singular personality. A virtuoso with the brush, he amassed a large fortune and married a wealthy heiress named Emma Lamm; when he came to build this gigantic chalet, which he called Zorngården, his intention was to show the world that he had well and truly arrived. A *bon vivant*, a patron of the arts, a collector of old silver, a tireless traveller and a particular lover of pretty women, Anders Zorn died on 22 August 1920 surrounded by the treasures he had amassed. His wife later bequeathed the house and its collections to the Swedish state, and ever since admirers of Zorn have been going there to admire them.

LEFT: *A bottle of "Caloric Punch" awaits guests on the covered terrace.*
ABOVE: *The painter's initials against a key-hole.*

LINKS: *Auf der über-dachten Terrasse erwar-tet der »Caloric Punch« die Gäste.*
OBEN: *Die Initiale des Malers ziert jetzt ein Türschloss.*

A GAUCHE: *Le «Caloric Punch» attend les invités sur la terrasse couverte.*
CI-DESSUS: *L'initiale du peintre orne mainte-nant une serrure.*

Das Haus des Malers Anders Zorn (1860–1920) ist mittlerweile ein Museum, aber der Geist des Künstlers ist in diesem imposanten Gebäude überall gegenwärtig. Zorn, der der leidenschaftlichen Beziehung zwischen einer jungen Schwedin und einem deutschen Bierbrauer entstammte, legte bald schon ein bemerkenswertes Talent fürs Zeichnen an den Tag und machte nach seinem Studium an der Stockholmer Kunstakademie eine steile Karriere. Man braucht heute nur sein Selbstportrait im roten Anzug anzusehen und das Augenmerk auf seinen mächtigen kantigen Kopf mit dem gebieterischen Blick zu richten, um die eindrucksvolle Persönlichkeit des Künstlers zu erfassen. Dieser Virtuose des Pinsels häufte, was nicht verwunderlich ist, Reichtümer an, heiratete eine reiche Erbin, Emma Lamm, und zeigte der Welt mit dem Bau der riesigen Villa, die er Zorngården taufte, wozu es ein durchaus bescheidener Sohn aus Dalarna bringen konnte. Der Lebemann, Mäzen, Sammler von Silberarbeiten, rastlose Reisende und große Liebhaber hübscher Frauen starb am 22. August 1920. Seine Frau vermachte das Haus und die Sammlungen dem Staat. Seither ist es Zorns Bewunderern vergönnt, sich hier von den Reichtümern eines unvergleichlichen Künstlers hinreißen zu lassen.

The property of Zorngården, built between 1895 and 1910, includes the house of the painter's grandparents, which Zorn had moved to Mora lock, stock and barrel.

Zorngården, erbaut von 1895 bis 1910, umfasst auch das Haus der Großeltern, eine bescheidene Bauernkate, die Zorn erwarb und nach Mora transportieren ließ.

Zorngården, construit entre 1895 et 1910, renferme aussi la maison de ses grands-parents, une modeste ferme qu'il acheta et fit transporter à Mora.

La maison du peintre Anders Zorn (1860–1920) est devenue un musée, mais l'esprit du peintre est si présent dans cette demeure imposante, que l'on s'attend à tout moment à voir sa silhouette robuste apparaître dans l'embrasure d'une porte. Zorn, fruit d'une liaison passionnée entre une jeune Suédoise et un brasseur allemand, fit très tôt preuve d'un talent remarquable pour le dessin et, après ses études aux Beaux-Arts de Stockholm, sa renommée et sa carrière montèrent en flèche. De nos jours, il suffit de regarder son autoportrait en costume rouge, d'observer sa tête puissante et carrée et son regard impérieux pour saisir la personnalité impressionnante de l'artiste. Ce virtuose du pinceau, nul ne s'en étonnera, amassa des fortunes, épousa une riche héritière, Emma Lamm, et, en construisant cet énorme chalet baptisé Zorngården, il montra au monde qu'un bien modeste natif de Dalécarlie pouvait atteindre le sommet de sa profession. Bon vivant, mécène, collectionneur d'argenterie, voyageur sans repos et grand amateur de jolies femmes, il mourut, entouré de ses trésors, le 22 août 1920. Son épouse légua la maison et ses collections à l'Etat et depuis, les admirateurs de Zorn peuvent s'émerveiller des richesses d'un artiste sans pareil.

The kitchen sideboard with its cargo of blue and white dishes.

Die große Anrichte in der Küche mit blau-weißen Tellern.

Le grand buffet de cuisine accueille des assiettes bleues et blanches.

FACING PAGE: *the door leading through to the covered terrace.*

ABOVE AND RIGHT: *Zorn's studio, in a wooden building that dates from the Middle Ages, was reconstructed beside his house. The painter's easel and smock are exactly as he left them.*

LINKE SEITE: *die Tür zur überdachten Terrasse.*

OBEN UND RECHTS: *Zorns Atelier befindet sich in einem Holzschuppen aus dem Mittelalter, der neben seinem Haus wiederaufgebaut wurde. Staffelei und Malerkittel sind noch an Ort und Stelle.*

PAGE DE GAUCHE: *la porte qui donne sur la terrasse couverte.*

CI-DESSUS ET À DROITE: *L'atelier de Zorn se trouve dans un bâtiment en bois datant du Moyen Age et construit à l'ombre de sa maison. Son chevalet et sa blouse de peintre n'ont pas changé de place.*

ABOVE: *This 30-foot-high space offers a blend of the rural architecture of Dalecarlia with the comfort of a traditional cottage.*

RIGHT: *In its time, this magnificent cooking stove was the last word in domestic fittings.*

FACING PAGE: *The painter and his wife came to this corner to relax and talk. The rectangular picture is typical of the folk painting of Dalecarlia, a genre of which Zorn was a passionate collector.*

OBEN: *Der elf Meter hohe Raum verbindet die rustikale Architektur der Provinz Dalarna mit dem Komfort eines traditionellen »Cottage«.*

RECHTS: *Der schöne Küchenherd bot zur damaligen Zeit ein Maximum an Komfort!*

RECHTE SEITE: *Hier kamen der Maler und seine Frau zusammen, um sich zu unterhalten oder zu entspannen. Das querformatige Gemälde ist typisch für die volkstümliche Malerei aus der Provinz Dalarna, die Zorn mit Leidenschaft sammelte.*

CI-DESSUS: *Cet espace haut de onze mètres sous les combles marie l'architecture rustique de Dalécarlie et le confort du «cottage» traditionnel.*

A DROITE: *La belle cuisinière était à l'époque le summum du confort ménager!*

PAGE DE DROITE: *Le peintre et sa femme se retrouvaient ici pour discuter ou se détendre. Le tableau rectangulaire est typique de la peinture folklorique de Dalécarlie que Zorn collectionnait avec passion.*

ABOVE: *Emma Zorn's bedroom: a Gustavian bed with a baldachin, and an Empire chest of drawers. After becoming blind, the painter's wife spent her last years in this room.*
RIGHT: *Anders Zorn's bedroom. On the Gustavian bed is a silk quilted bedspread.*
FACING PAGE: *Mrs Zorn loved the Gustavian style. Her small green salon is full of understated elegance, with fine chairs, console table, gilt looking-glass and family portraits.*

OBEN: *Im Zimmer von Emma Zorn fallen das Bett und die Kommode ins Auge. Nachdem sie erblindet war, verbrachte sie hier ihre letzten Lebensjahre.*
RECHTS: *das Zimmer von Anders Zorn mit dem gustavianischen Himmelbett, auf dem eine Seidendecke liegt.*
RECHTE SEITE: *Emma Zorn bewunderte den gustavianischen Stil. Der kleine grüne Salon mit seinen Sesseln, seinem Konsoltisch, seinem vergoldeten Spiegel und den Familienportraits verkörpert ihn aufs Eleganteste.*

CI-DESSUS: *Dans la chambre d'Emma Zorn, le lit et la commode Empire attirent l'attention. Devenue aveugle, l'épouse du peintre passa ici les dernières années de sa vie.*
A DROITE: *la chambre d'Anders Zorn avec son lit à baldaquin gustavien et son «quilt» en soie.*
PAGE DE DROITE: *Madame Zorn adorait le style gustavien et le petit salon vert est des plus élégants grâce à ses sièges, sa console, son miroir doré et ses portraits de famille.*

LEFT: *The console and mirror in the bathroom are pure 18th century, but the heating elements and the astonishing radiator show that the Zorns were not averse to basic modern comforts, either.*

FACING PAGE: *This guest bedroom, entirely furnished in the Gustavian style, was reserved for Prince Eugene, a great friend of the family.*

LINKS: *Konsoltisch und Spiegel des Badezimmers sind zwar aus dem 18. Jahrhundert, doch lassen die Heizelemente und der erstaunliche Radiator erkennen, dass die Familie »modernen« Komfort nicht verschmähte.*

RECHTE SEITE: *Das ganz im gustavianischen Stil möblierte Gästezimmer war für einen großen Freund der Familie reserviert: Prinz Eugen.*

A GAUCHE: *Si la console et le miroir de la salle de bains sont pur 18ᵉ, les éléments de chauffage et l'étonnant radiateur nous révèlent que la famille ne dédaignait pas le confort «moderne».*

PAGE DE DROITE: *La chambre d'amis, entièrement meublée dans le style gustavien, était réservée à un grand ami de la famille: le Prince Eugène.*

$\mathcal{L}$EUFSTA HERRGÅRD

Uppland

The castle of Leufsta, in the heart of the picturesque village of Lovstabruk, stands at the heart of an ensemble of buildings in a park of near-perfect symmetry. Built in 1720 to replace a feudal manor destroyed by invading Russian troops, Leufsta herrgård was designed to reflect the power of its owner, Baron Charles De Geer (1720–1778). His ancestor Louis De Geer, a wealthy Dutch merchant, bought the forges for which the region is famous and recruited a large number of artisans from Wallonia to work in them. To show off his fortune, the baron commissioned the famous architect Jean Eric Rehn to decorate his castle, and Leufsta owes its wonderful elegance to Rehn's talent. Apart from the small, intimate salons in which the ambience is mostly Louis XV, the *pièce de résistance* is without doubt the splendid panelled dining room with its tones of grey, white and gold, the walls of which are hung with portraits of ancestors. In the basement, the kitchens and cellars have remained unaltered for nearly two hundred years; all in all, thanks to the care of the present owners (Baron and Baroness Louis De Geer), Leufsta has withstood the passage of time without a blemish.

LEFT: *In the kitchen, the old telephone is still in its place next to the door.*
ABOVE: *a magnifying glass and a book left on the chaise longue.*

LINKS: *Das alte Telefon in der Küche hat seinen Platz neben der Tür behalten.*
OBEN: *ein auf dem Sofa abgelegtes Buch mit Lupe.*

A GAUCHE: *Dans la cuisine, le vieux téléphone a gardé sa place près de la porte.*
CI-DESSUS: *un livre et une loupe abandonnés sur une chaise-longue.*

In the kitchen, preparations for dinner are under way.

In der Küche scheint alles zur Zubereitung eines Mahls bereit.

Dans la cuisine, tout semble prêt à la préparation d'un repas.

Schloss Leufsta, im Herzen der malerischen Ortschaft Lövstabruk gelegen, erhebt sich inmitten eines Gebäudeensembles und eines Parks, der durch seine vollendet symmetrische Anlage besticht. 1720 anstelle eines von russischen Truppen zerstörten Herrenguts errichtet, spiegelte Leufsta herrgård die Macht seines Besitzers, des Barons Charles De Geer (1720–1778) wider. Dessen Ahnherr Louis De Geer, ein steinreicher niederländischer Händler, hatte die Eisenhütten, die das Ansehen der Region ausmachten, aufgekauft und zahlreiche Werkleute aus der Wallonie angeworben. Um seinen Reichtum zu veranschaulichen, vertraute der Baron die Ausgestaltung des Schlosses dem berühmten Architekten Jean Eric Rehn an, dem Leufsta die schlichte Eleganz verdankt. Mit Ausnahme der intimen kleinen Salons, in denen ein vom französischen Louis-XV-Stil inspiriertes Ambiente herrscht, bildet das Hauptstück zweifelsohne der prächtige Speisesaal, der in Grau-, Weiß- und Goldtönen getäfelt und mit Familienbildnissen geschmückt ist. Die Küchen in den Gewölbekellern sind seit fast zwei Jahrhunderten unverändert geblieben und dank der konservatorischen Sorgfalt der derzeitigen Besitzer, Baron und Baronin Louis De Geer, ist Leufsta um nichts gealtert.

Le château de Leufsta, situé au cœur du village pittoresque de Lövstabruk, se dresse au centre d'un ensemble de bâtiments et d'un parc dont on admire la symétrie parfaite. Construit en 1720 pour remplacer une demeure seigneuriale détruite par les troupes ennemies russes, Leufsta herrgård reflétait le pouvoir de son propriétaire, le baron Charles De Geer (1720–1778). Son ancêtre Louis De Geer, un richissime marchand néerlandais, avait acheté les forges qui faisaient la réputation de la région et avait recruté un grand nombre d'artisans venus de Wallonie. Pour montrer sa fortune, le baron confia la décoration du château au célèbre architecte Jean Eric Rehn et Leufsta doit son élégance sobre au talent exceptionnel de celui-ci. Excepté les petits salons intimes où règne une ambiance inspirée par le goût français sous le règne de Louis XV, la pièce de résistance est sans aucun doute la splendide salle à manger lambrissée aux tons de gris, blanc et or et ornée de portraits de famille. Dans les sous-sols, les cuisines-caves voûtées n'ont pas changé depuis bientôt deux siècles et, grâce à l'esprit conservateur des actuels propriétaires – le baron et la baronne Louis De Geer –, Leufsta n'a pas pris une ride.

Leufsta herrgård, built in 1720, is surrounded by beautiful parkland.

Leufsta herrgård, 1720 erbaut, liegt in einem wundervollen Park.

Leufsta herrgård, construit en 1720, est entouré d'un parc magnifique.

ABOVE: *The elegant décor of the salon was designed by the architect Jean Eric Rehn (1717–1793), who studied in Paris.*
RIGHT: *trompe-l'œil décor and rich furniture and pictures in the antechamber.*
FACING PAGE: *trompe-l'œil panels and 'sculpted' garlands on the walls of the antechamber.*

OBEN: *Die elegante Ausstattung des großen Salons hat der Architekt Jean Eric Rehn (1717–1793) entworfen, der sein Studium großenteils in Paris absolvierte.*
RECHTS: *Das Vorzimmer besticht durch sein Trompe-l'Œil-Dekor und die üppige Ausstattung mit Möbeln und Gemälden.*
RECHTE SEITE: *Täfelungen in Trompel'Œil-Technik und »geschnitzte« Girlanden an den Wänden des Vorzimmers.*

CI-DESSUS: *L'architecte Jean Eric Rehn (1717–1793) a conçu le décor élégant du grand salon. Il avait fait une grande partie de ses études à Paris.*
A DROITE: *L'antichambre est caractérisée par son décor en trompe-l'œil et par la richesse de son mobilier et de ses tableaux.*
PAGE DE DROITE: *lambris en trompe-l'œil et guirlandes «sculptées» pour les murs de l'antichambre.*

The walls of the kitchen show their age, but the red-gold coppers are still shiny and ready for use.

Die Küchenwände sind vom Alter gezeichnet, aber das kupferne Koch-geschirr funkelt so feurig, als warte es auf seinen Einsatz.

Les murs de la cuisine sont vétustes, mais la batterie en cuivre rou-geâtre brille de tous ses feux comme si elle attendait de faire ses preuves.

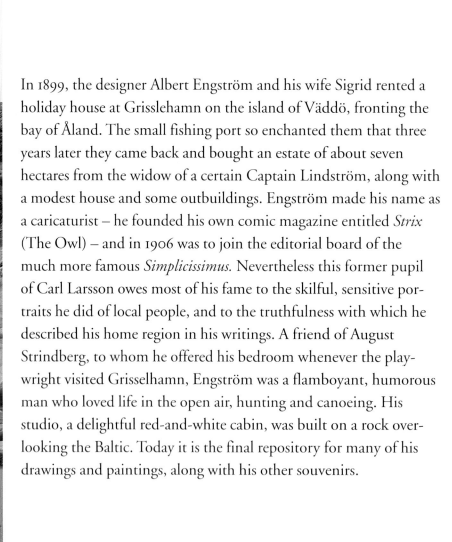

$\mathcal{A}$LBERT ENGSTRÖM

Uppland

In 1899, the designer Albert Engström and his wife Sigrid rented a holiday house at Grisslehamn on the island of Väddö, fronting the bay of Åland. The small fishing port so enchanted them that three years later they came back and bought an estate of about seven hectares from the widow of a certain Captain Lindström, along with a modest house and some outbuildings. Engström made his name as a caricaturist – he founded his own comic magazine entitled *Strix* (The Owl) – and in 1906 was to join the editorial board of the much more famous *Simplicissimus.* Nevertheless this former pupil of Carl Larsson owes most of his fame to the skilful, sensitive portraits he did of local people, and to the truthfulness with which he described his home region in his writings. A friend of August Strindberg, to whom he offered his bedroom whenever the playwright visited Grisselhamn, Engström was a flamboyant, humorous man who loved life in the open air, hunting and canoeing. His studio, a delightful red-and-white cabin, was built on a rock overlooking the Baltic. Today it is the final repository for many of his drawings and paintings, along with his other souvenirs.

PREVIOUS PAGES: *Albert Engström's promontory studio on Väddö Island, confronting the changing moods of the sea.*
LEFT: *a view of Åland Bay.*

VORHERGEHENDE DOPPELSEITE: *Das Atelier von Albert Engström auf einer Landzunge der Insel Väddö trotzt den wechselnden Stimmungen des Meeres.*
LINKS: *Ansicht der Bucht von Åland.*

DOUBLE PAGE PRÉCÉDENTE: *L'atelier d'Albert Engström, construit sur une pointe de l'île de Väddö, brave les humeurs changeantes de la mer.*
A GAUCHE: *une vue de la baie d'Åland.*

The artist Albert
Engström.

Der Künstler Albert
Engström.

L'artiste Albert Eng-
ström.

1899 mieteten der Zeichner Albert Engström und seine Frau
Sigrid ein Ferienhaus in Grisslehamn auf der Insel Väddö
gegenüber der Bucht von Åland. Der kleine Fischerhafen ent-
zückte sie so sehr, dass sie 1902 ein fast sieben Hektar großes
Grundstück erwarben, auf dem ein bescheidenes Haus sowie
einige Nebengebäude standen. Engström hatte sich einen
Namen als Karikaturist gemacht: Er hatte seine eigene Satire-
zeitschrift »Strix« (Uhu) gegründet und trat 1906 der Redak-
tion des berühmten »Simplicissimus« bei. Doch verdankt der
ehemalige Schüler von Carl Larsson seinen Ruf vor allem den
ausgesprochen virtuosen und feinfühligen Portraits, die er von
den Bewohnern der Region anfertigte, und der Wahrhaftig-
keit, mit der er sie in seinen Schriften verewigte. August
Strindberg, mit dem er befreundet war, verbrachte gelegentlich
ein paar Tage in Grisslehamn und wohnte dann in Engströms
Zimmer. Sein Atelier ließ sich der brillante Künstler, der für
seinen Humor bekannt war und das Leben im Freien, die Jagd
und Ausflüge mit dem Kanu liebte, auf einem Felsen mit Blick
auf die Ostsee bauen. Heute dient dieses faszinierende Häus-
chen mit seinem rotweißen Anstrich als letzter Aufbewah-
rungsort für seine Zeichnungen, Gemälde und Andenken.

En 1899, le dessinateur Albert Engström et sa femme Sigrid
louèrent une maison de vacances à Grisslehamn dans l'île de
Väddö, face à la baie d'Åland. Ce petit port de pêche les char-
ma à tel point qu'ils achetèrent trois ans plus tard à la veuve
d'un certain capitaine Lindström un domaine de près de sept
hectares où se trouvaient une modeste maison et quelques
dépendances. Engström s'était fait un nom comme caricaturis-
te – il avait fondé son propre magazine comique «Strix» (Le
Hibou) et devait adhérer en 1906 à la rédaction du célèbre
«Simplicissimus» –, mais cet ancien élève de Carl Larsson doit
avant tout sa renommée aux portraits pleins de virtuosité et de
sensibilité qu'il fit des habitants de la région et à la véracité
avec laquelle il immortalisa ceux-ci dans ses écrits. Ami d'August Strindberg – qui passait parfois quelques jours à Grisslehamn et logeait dans la chambre d'Engström –, ce flamboyant
artiste plein d'humour qui adorait la vie au grand air, la chasse
et les randonnées en canoë, se fit construire un atelier sur un
rocher face à la Baltique. De nos jours, ce fascinant cabanon
peint en rouge et blanc est devenu l'ultime refuge de ses dessins, de ses tableaux et de ses souvenirs.

The painter's box of oils,
placed on a reclining
armchair.

Der Farbkasten des
Künstlers auf einem
Klappstuhl.

La boîte à couleurs du
peintre, posée sur un
fauteuil à dossier incli-
nable.

FACING PAGE: *some of Engström's painting equipment, with one of his last pictures propped on the easel.*
RIGHT: *The big corner mirror was used for sketching models in profile and for outlining self-portraits.*
FOLLOWING PAGES: *The little bridge leads across the stream to the house.*

LINKE SEITE: *Engströms Gerätschaften und eines seiner letzten Gemälde auf der Staffelei.*
RECHTS: *Der große Eckspiegel diente dazu, Modelle im Profil zu skizzieren oder Selbstportraits zu fertigen.*
FOLGENDE DOPPELSEITE: *Die kleine Brücke über den Fluss führt zum Haus.*

PAGE DE GAUCHE: *les ustensiles d'Engström et un de ses derniers tableaux sur le chevalet.*
A DROITE: *Le grand miroir d'angle servait jadis à croquer les modèles de profil et à brosser des autoportraits.*
DOUBLE PAGE SUIVANTE: *Le petit pont qui enjambe le ruisseau mène vers la maison.*

FACING PAGE: *The staircase leading to the bedrooms has a brightly-painted fretwork banister.*
ABOVE: *The Engströms' house has become a museum, but the painter's admirers can still sense its timeless, living atmosphere.*
RIGHT: *The painter's bedroom is just as it always was – Engström always relinquished his chamber to his friend August Strindberg when he came to visit.*

LINKE SEITE: *Die Treppe zu den Schlafzimmern ziert eine mit der Laubsäge gearbeitete Balustrade in kräftigen Farben.*
OBEN: *Das Haus der Engströms ist heute ein Museum, aber die Bewunderer des Malers begegnen darin einer zeitlos lebendigen Stimmung.*
RECHTS: *Das Schlafzimmer des Malers ist vollständig erhalten. Er trat es seinem Freund August Strindberg ab, wenn dieser ihn besuchte.*

PAGE DE GAUCHE: *L'escalier qui conduit aux chambres à coucher est orné d'une balustrade fraisée aux couleurs vives.*
CI-DESSUS: *La maison des Engström est devenue un musée, mais les admirateurs du peintre y trouvent une ambiance vivante et intemporelle.*
A DROITE: *La chambre à coucher du peintre est restée intacte. Il la cédait à son ami August Strindberg quand celui-ci lui rendait visite.*

$\mathcal{L}$INNÉS HAMMARBY

Uppland

"A great man may be born in a small cottage," wrote the famous naturalist Carl von Linné (1707–1778), also known as Carolus Linnaeus. He knew what he was talking about, having been born in just such a modest house at Råshult in Småland, "at the height of the spring season, when the cuckoo was heralding the advent of summer". Linnaeus liked to say that he became a botanist in his mother's womb, because during her pregnancy she never stopped gazing at the pretty garden that her husband, the local pastor, had created around their house. She couldn't have known that her son would become one of the world's greatest scholars, nor that his travels to Lapland, his time in Holland and his expeditions around his own native Sweden would strengthen his love of nature and his conviction that man is an animal just like all the others. In 1758 Linnaeus, who was said by some to have "completed the work of God" by giving scientific names to animals and plants, bought himself a charming red-painted house at Hammarby. Here, in the green countryside south east of Uppsala, he created a garden filled with aromatic herbs and spent several peaceful years completing the final edition of his *Systema Naturae*.

PREVIOUS PAGES: *the glorious view from Linnaeus's garden.*
LEFT: *Blue cotton curtains protect the interior of the house from the rays of the midday sun.*

VORHERGEHENDE DOPPELSEITE: *Im Garten genießt man eine großartige Aussicht auf die herrliche Landschaft.*
LINKS: *Vorhänge aus blauem Baumwoll-Voile schützen die Innenräume vor der Mittagssonne.*

DOUBLE PAGE PRÉCÉDENTE: *Du jardin, on a une vue imprenable sur le paysage magnifique.*
A GAUCHE: *Des rideaux en voile de coton bleu protègent l'intérieur contre le soleil de midi.*

Linnaeus's sunlit stoop.

*Der sonnige Eingangs-
bereich lädt zur Ent-
spannung ein.*

*Le perron ensoleillé
invite à la détente.*

»Ein großer Mann kann in einer bescheidenen Strohhütte zur Welt kommen«, schrieb der berühmte Naturforscher Carl von Linné (1707–1778), der sich auch Carolus Linnaeus nannte. Er wusste, wovon er sprach, denn er wurde in einer Hütte in Råshult im Småland geboren, »mitten im Frühjahr, zu dem Zeitpunkt, als der Kuckuck die Ankunft des Sommers verkündete«. Linné hat oft behauptet, er sei im Leib seiner Mutter zum Botaniker geworden, die während ihrer Schwangerschaft nie den Blick von dem Garten gelassen habe, den ihr Ehemann, der Pastor des Weilers, nahe beim Haus angelegt hatte. Sie wusste noch nicht, dass ihr Sohn zu einem der größten Wissenschaftler der Welt heranwachsen würde und dass seine Reisen nach Lappland, sein Aufenthalt in den Niederlanden und seine Studienfahrten durchs eigene Land seine Naturliebe stärken und seine Überzeugung »homo est animal« – der Mensch ist ein Tier – festigen sollten. Linnaeus, von dem es heißt, er habe das Werk Gottes vollendet, indem er den Pflanzen und Tieren ihre wissenschaftlichen Namen gab, kaufte 1758 ein reizvolles Anwesen in Hammarby im Südosten von Uppsala. Hier legte er einen Garten mit aromatischen Kräutern an und brachte die letzte Ausgabe seines »Systema Naturae« zu Ende.

«Un grand homme peut naître dans une modeste chaumière» a écrit le célèbre naturaliste Carl von Linné (1707–1778), dit aussi Carolus Linnaeus. Il parlait en connaissance de cause, lui qui était né dans une chaumière à Råshult dans le Småland «à l'apogée du printemps et au moment où le coucou annonçait l'arrivée de l'été». Linné prétendait souvent qu'il était devenu botaniste dans le ventre de sa mère qui, pendant sa grossesse, n'aurait pas quitté des yeux le joli petit jardin que son mari, le pasteur du hameau, avait créé près de la maison. Elle ne savait pas encore que son fils deviendrait un des plus grands savants du monde et que ses voyages en Laponie, son séjour aux Pays-Bas et ses voyages d'étude à travers son propre pays renforceraient son amour pour la nature et sa conviction que «Homo est animal» – l'homme est un animal. Linnaeus qui, selon certains, avait achevé la tâche de Dieu en donnant un nom scientifique aux animaux et aux plantes, acheta en 1758 une charmante propriété à Hammarby, au sud-est d'Uppsala. C'est ici, dans cette modeste maison rouge entourée d'un paysage verdoyant qu'il créa un jardin planté d'herbes aromatiques et qu'il passa quelques années paisibles en achevant la dernière édition de son «Systema Naturae».

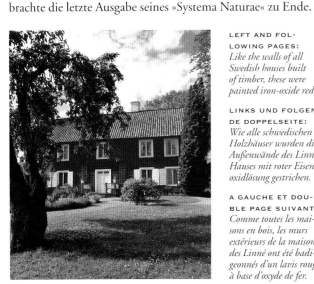

LEFT AND FOL-
LOWING PAGES:
*Like the walls of all
Swedish houses built
of timber, these were
painted iron-oxide red.*

LINKS UND FOLGEN-
DE DOPPELSEITE:
*Wie alle schwedischen
Holzhäuser wurden die
Außenwände des Linné-
Hauses mit roter Eisen-
oxidlösung gestrichen.*

A GAUCHE ET DOU-
BLE PAGE SUIVANTE:
*Comme toutes les mai-
sons en bois, les murs
extérieurs de la maison
des Linné ont été badi-
geonnés d'un lavis rouge
à base d'oxyde de fer.*

ABOVE: *Linnaeus's bedroom is papered with botanical illustrations published by Burmannius. The portrait on the left is that of the great scientist himself; the one on the right represents Carl Gustav Tessin.*

RIGHT: *in the antechamber, a portrait of Sara Morea in her wedding dress, by Johan Henrik Scheffel (1739).*

FACING PAGE: *The delicately-striped flowered wallpaper is typical of the period. The 18th-century deal chair is painted in trompe-l'œil imitation hardwood.*

OBEN: *Linnés Zimmer ist mit botanischen Abbildungen tapeziert. Burmannius, der sie publizierte, schaut auf die Besucher herab. Das Portrait rechts zeigt Carl Gustav Tessin.*

RECHTS: *im Vorzimmer ein Portrait von Sara Morea in Brauttracht, gemalt 1739 von Johan Henrik Scheffel.*

RECHTE SEITE: *Die gestreifte Tapete mit Blumenmotiven ist typisch für die Epoche. Der Kiefernholzstuhl aus dem 18. Jahrhundert wurde mit einem Trompe-l'Œil-Anstrich versehen, der ein Edelholz imitiert.*

CI-DESSUS: *La chambre de Linné est tapissée d'illustrations botaniques publiées par Burmannius. Dans son cadre doré, à gauche, il semble observer les visiteurs. Le portrait à droite représente Carl Gustav Tessin.*

A DROITE: *dans l'antichambre, un portrait de Sara Morea en mariée, peint par Johan Henrik Scheffel en 1739.*

PAGE DE DROITE: *Le papier peint rayé à délicat motif floral est typique de l'époque. La chaise 18ᵉ en pin est peinte en trompe-l'œil imitant un bois précieux.*

FACING PAGE: *the walls of the antechamber, with flowered paper and a trompe-l'œil panel decorated with flowers, scrolls and shell-shapes.*
RIGHT: *In the antechamber, a canapé upholstered in yellow linen with a portrait of Linnaeus overhead. The bed next door dates from the Gustavian period.*

LINKE SEITE: *die Vorzimmerwände mit Blumentapete und einem Trompe-l'Œil, das eine mit Blumen, Zierleisten und Muschelwerk geschmückte Täfelung vortäuscht.*
RECHTS: *Im Vorzimmer, das ein Portrait des Hausherrn beherrscht, haben die Linnés ein mit gelbem Leinen bezogenes Kanapee aufgestellt. Das Bett im Schlafzimmer stammt aus der gustavianischen Epoche.*

PAGE DE GAUCHE: *les murs de l'antichambre avec papier peint à fleurs et trompe-l'œil imitant un lambris décoré de fleurs, de cartouches et de coquilles.*
A DROITE: *Dans l'antichambre dominée par un portrait du maître de maison, les Linné ont installé un canapé habillé de lin jaune. Le lit de la chambre à coucher date de l'époque gustavienne.*

SKOKLOSTER SLOTT

Mälaren

In 1654, Marshal Carl Gustav Wrangel (1613–1676) began the construction of Skokloster Castle, thereby adding a new architectural
gem to his impressive collection of castles and manor houses. Count
Wrangel was an important man who had covered himself with glory
and honours, including the titles of Governor of Pomerania, General of the Swedish Crown, and Grand Admiral. But apart from his
political power, this colourful character was famous for his vast collection of furniture, arms, armour, earthenware, carpets, fabrics,
silver, books, paintings and old glass. Skokloster, it is clear, was
deliberately planned as a showcase for Wrangel's treasures, and
today anyone who visits his vast salons with their walls upholstered
in Cordoba leather can easily form an idea of his uneven, luxurious
taste. Beneath the baroque stucco ceilings are an assortment of
richly-draped four-poster beds, life-size equestrian portraits, and
ivory-encrusted desks. There is even a fully-laid table in the purest
17th-century taste, which seems to await the arrival of the hearty
Count and his retinue.

*In one of the attic bed-
rooms, a striped linen
slip-cover protects the
delicate upholstery of a
carved wooden chair.*

*In einem der Zimmer
unter dem Dachstuhl
schützt ein Bezug aus
gestreiftem Leinen das
empfindliche Polster
eines beschnitzten Holz-
stuhls.*

*Dans une des chambres
sous les combles, une
housse en toile rayée
protège le rembourrage
délicat d'une chaise en
bois sculpté.*

1654 gab der Marschall Carl Gustav Wrangel (1613–1676) grünes Licht für den Bau des Schlosses Skokloster, womit er seine eindrucksvolle Sammlung von Schlössern und Herrengütern erweiterte. Graf Wrangel war eine bedeutende Persönlichkeit von erklecklichem Ruhm und Titeln, darunter der des Statthalters von Pommern, des Generals der schwedischen Krone und des Großadmirals. Abgesehen von seiner politischen Macht aber war dieser temperamentvolle Mann dafür berühmt, dass er eine umfangreiche Sammlung von Möbeln, Waffen, Rüstungen, Porzellan, Teppichen, Stoffen, Silberwaren, Büchern, Gemälden und historischen Glasarbeiten zusammengetragen hatte. Skokloster war als ein Schatzkästchen geplant, in dem die Reichtümer Wrangels zur Geltung kommen sollten, und wer heute durch die weitläufigen, mit Leder ausgekleideten Salons spaziert, gewinnt eine Vorstellung von seiner Vorliebe für prächtigen Raumschmuck. Unter stuckverzierten Barockdecken finden sich reich drapierte Himmelbetten, Reiterstandbilder in Lebensgröße, elfenbeinbesetzte Sekretäre und sogar eine ganz im Stil des 17. Jahrhunderts gedeckte Tafel, die den Grafen und seinen Hofstaat zu erwarten scheint.

A stone bust occupies a niche in the vaulted entrance hall.

Eine Steinbüste schmückt in der überwölbten Eingangshalle eine Nische.

Dans l'entrée voûtée, un buste en pierre décore une niche.

En 1654, le maréchal Carl Gustav Wrangel (1613–1676) donna le feu vert à la construction du château de Skokloster, ajoutant un nouveau joyau architectural à sa collection impressionnante de châteaux et de manoirs. Le comte Wrangel était un personnage important, couvert de gloire et de titres parmi lesquels il comptait celui de gouverneur de Poméranie, de général de la couronne de Suède et de grand amiral. Mais en dehors de son pouvoir politique, ce personnage haut en couleurs fut également célèbre pour avoir réuni une vaste collection de meubles, d'armes, d'armures, de faïences, de tapis, de tissus, de pièces d'argenterie, de livres, de tableaux et de verrerie ancienne. Skokloster, c'est évident, était conçu comme un écrin destiné à mettre en valeur les richesses de Wrangel et, de nos jours, ceux qui traversent les vastes salons tapissés de cuir de Cordoue, peuvent se faire une idée de son goût inégalé du faste. Sous des plafonds baroques ornés de stuc on trouve des lits à baldaquin richement drapés, des portraits équestres grandeur nature, des cabinets-secrétaires incrustés d'ivoire et même une table dressée dans le plus pur goût 17ᵉ qui semble attendre le comte et sa cour au robuste appétit.

LEFT: *In an octagonal salon decorated à l'antique, white marble effigies of various members of the Wrangel dynasty surround a magnificent neo-classical statue of Mars, the god of war.*

FACING PAGE: *Portraits of ancestors, proverbs in Latin and Swedish, trompe-l'œil panels and faux marbre cover the walls of the gallery.*

LINKS: *In einem nach antikem Muster gestalteten achteckigen Saal stehen rings um einen klassizistischen Kriegsgott weiße Marmorstatuen verschiedener Persönlichkeiten der Dynastie Wrangel.*

RECHTE SEITE: *Ahnenportraits, Spruchweisheiten in lateinischer wie schwedischer Sprache, Täfelungen in Trompe-l'Œil-Manier sowie Marmorimitat* schmücken die Wände der Galerie.

A GAUCHE: *Dans un salon octogonal, décoré à l'antique, des effigies en marbre blanc de différentes figures de la dynastie des Wrangel, entourent un magnifique dieu de la guerre néoclassique.*

PAGE DE DROITE: *Des portraits d'ancêtres, des proverbes en latin et en suédois et un trompe-l'œil de lambris et de faux marbre décorent les parois de la galerie.*

RIGHT: *In the same salon, the trompe-l'œil frescoes done in a cameo of different whites imitate bas reliefs and niches occupied by Winged Victories. The neo-Gothic chairs date from the first half of the 19th century.*

RECHTS: *Im selben Salon imitieren weiß in weiß gehaltene Trompe-l'Œil-Fresken Flachreliefs und mit Siegesgöttinnen geschmückte Nischen. Die neugotischen Stühle stammen aus der ersten Hälfte des 19. Jahrhunderts.*

A DROITE: *Dans ce même salon, les fresques en trompe-l'œil exécutées en un camaïeu de blancs, imitent des bas-reliefs et des niches ornées de victoires. Les sièges néogothiques datent de la première moitié du 19ᵉ siècle.*

ABOVE: *The state bedroom is sumptuously appointed, but the real focus of attention here is the four-poster bed draped with gold-spangled crimson silk.*

RIGHT: *a chair, upholstered with red and white striped linen, standing in a window embrasure.*

FACING PAGE: *a four-poster in one of the bedrooms, draped with the same shimmering red as the table and the windows.*

OBEN: *Bei aller Pracht des repräsentativen Schlafraums – Blickfang ist das Himmelbett, drapiert mit karmesinroter Seide, die mit Goldpailletten bestickt ist.*

RECHTS: *In der Fensternische steht ein mit rotweiß gestreiftem Leinen bezogener Stuhl.*

RECHTE SEITE: *In einem der Schlafzimmer verbindet ein schillerndes Rot Himmelbett, Tisch und Vorhänge.*

CI-DESSUS: *La chambre à coucher d'apparat est somptueuse, mais c'est le lit à baldaquin drapé de soie cramoisie brodée de paillettes dorées, qui attire toute l'attention.*

A DROITE: *dans le renfoncement d'une fenêtre, une chaise housée de toile à rayures rouges et blanches.*

PAGE DE DROITE: *Dans une des chambres à coucher, un rouge chatoyant habille le lit à baldaquin, le jupon d'une table et les rideaux.*

LEFT: *In the attic rooms, frescoes create the illusion of a classical colonnade twined around with climbing plants.*
FACING PAGE: *The Wrangels appreciated good food – guests at their table could be sure of excellent wine, fruit, nuts, and an array of hot dishes that might include roast swan.*

LINKS: *In den Räumen unter dem Dach erzeugen Fresken die Illusion eines klassischen Säulengangs, der von Kletterpflanzen überwuchert wird.*
RECHTE SEITE: *Die Wrangels schätzten das pralle Leben und auf den mit erlesenen Speisen beladenen Tafeln fanden sich Früchte, Nüsse und Wein in Hülle und Fülle, wobei der berühmte gebratene Schwan nicht fehlen durfte.*

A GAUCHE: *Dans les salles aménagées sous les combles, les fresques créent l'illusion d'une colonnade classique envahie par des plantes grimpantes.*
PAGE DE DROITE: *Les Wrangel appréciaient la bonne chère et sur les tables chargées de mets exquis on trouvait souvent des fruits, des noix et du vin à profusion, et même le fameux rôti de cygne.*

ᴀLMARE STÄKET

Irène och Johan Seth

Mälaren

Almare Stäket stands at the top of a hill, one flank of which slopes down to the still waters of Lake Mälaren. It would make a perfect subject for a romantic painting, being a beautiful, austere house in a strategic site that once served as a retreat for a powerful archbishop. "Friherre" Jöran Gyllenstierna, who bought the property in 1642, added robust lines, but it was at the end of the 18th century, under Count Samuel af Ugglas, that Almare Stäket acquired its broad main building and the beautiful neo-classical gateway which embellishes the façade overlooking the lake. Several decades ago, the "herrgård" passed into the hands of Johan and Irène Seth. Their dream was to share the unique ambience of their house with paying guests, and in consequence they embarked on a restoration of great refinement which respected the authenticity of the interior without neglecting modern comforts. To spend a while in the company of this delightful family, to linger in the salon decorated by Masreliez or to sleep in a four-poster bed beside a tiled stove in one of the bedrooms, is an experience to treasure. Add the pleasures of the Seths' table, and of teatime in the lake pavilion – and there you have it: the portrait of Almare Stäket.

PREVIOUS PAGES: *behind the manor house, a 19th-century wooden pavilion by the lake.*
LEFT: *a 19th-century gilt-bronze candelabra beside one of the drawing room windows.*

VORHERGEHENDE DOPPELSEITE: *Am See hinter dem Gutshaus steht ein Holzpavillon aus dem 19. Jahrhundert.*
LINKS: *Vor einem der Fenster des Großen Salons wurde ein vergoldeter Bronzekandelaber aus dem 19. Jahrhundert aufgestellt.*

DOUBLE PAGE PRÉCÉDENTE: *Un pavillon en bois du 19ᵉ siècle près du lac qui se trouve derrière le manoir.*
A GAUCHE: *Un candélabre 19ᵉ en bronze doré est posé sur un meuble près d'une fenêtre du grand salon.*

Auf einem Hügel gelegen, der sanft zum Mälaren-See hin abfällt, scheint Almare Stäket geradewegs einem romantischen Gemälde entsprungen zu sein. Und doch hat dieses schöne Gebäude mit seinen strengen Formen sich als strategischer Ort erwiesen und einem mächtigen Erzbischof als Zuflucht gedient. Der »friherre« Jöran Gyllenstierna, der die Besitzung 1642 erwarb, verlieh ihr die robusten Formen, doch im ausgehenden 18. Jahrhundert wurde die Anlage unter dem Grafen Samuel af Ugglas um ein Wohnhaus und das bildschöne klassizistische Portal erweitert, das die zum See gelegene Fassade ziert. Vor ein paar Jahrzehnten ist das »herrgård« in die Hände von Johan und Irène Seth übergegangen, denen vorschwebte, das einzigartige Ambiente ihres Wohnsitzes mit zahlenden Gästen zu teilen. Deshalb nahmen sie eine Restaurierung vor, bei der die Authentizität der Interieurs gewahrt blieb, ohne Abstriche beim modernen Komfort zu machen. Eine Weile bei dieser gastlichen Familie zu verbringen und sich in einem von Masreliez ausgestatteten Salon aufzuhalten oder in einem Himmelbett zu schlafen, ist ein unvergessliches Erlebnis. Wenn wir noch die Tafelfreuden und den »Tee« im Seepavillon hinzunehmen, ist das Portrait von Almare Stäket komplett.

The main entrance to the manor was added at the end of the 18th century. The columns and architrave are of granite.

Das Portal des Schlosses wurde Ende des 18. Jahrhunderts angebaut. Säulen und Architrav sind aus Granit.

L'entrée principale du manoir a été ajoutée à la fin du 18ᵉ siècle. Les colonnes et l'architrave sont en granit.

Posé au sommet d'une colline dont un flanc descend en pente douce vers le miroir paisible du lac de Mälaren, Almare Stäket semble sorti tout droit d'un tableau romantique. Pourtant cette belle demeure aux lignes sévères s'est illustrée comme site stratégique et a servi de refuge à un archevêque puissant. Le «friherre» Jöran Gyllenstierna qui acheta la propriété en 1642 lui a donné ses formes robustes, mais c'est à la fin du 18ᵉ siècle, sous le comte Samuel af Ugglas, que la demeure s'enrichit d'un vaste corps de logis et du très beau portail néoclassique qui embellit la façade donnant sur le lac. Voilà plusieurs décennies que le «herrgård» est passé entre les mains de Johan et Irène Seth et comme ceux-ci rêvaient de partager l'ambiance unique de leur résidence avec des hôtes payants, ils ont entrepris une restauration très raffinée qui respecte l'authenticité des intérieurs, sans négliger le confort moderne. Passer un moment au sein de cette famille chaleureuse et séjourner dans un salon décoré à l'antique par Masreliez ou dormir dans un lit à baldaquin, blotti contre un poêle en faïence, sont des expériences mémorables. Ajoutons-y les plaisirs de la table ou le «thé» au pavillon du lac, et voilà brossé le portrait d'Almare Stäket.

An Empire marble bust, keeping an eye on things.

Eine Empire-Marmorbüste scheint zu beobachten, was in dem Raum vor sich geht.

Un buste en marbre Empire semble observer le va-et-vient.

PREVIOUS PAGES,
LEFT: *lake Mälaren
from the terrace.*
PREVIOUS PAGES,
RIGHT: *The "Pompei-
ian" décor of the salon
dates from 1800, as does
the crystal chandelier.
The glass cabinet con-
tains a collection of
antique fans.*
RIGHT: *The tiled stove
dates from the reign of
Gustav IV but its stylis-
tic ancestry doubtless
goes much farther back.
It was probably built
circa 1800.*

VORHERGEHENDE
DOPPELSEITE,
LINKS: *Blick vom Ein-
gangsvorplatz auf den
Mälaren-See.*
VORHERGEHENDE
DOPPELSEITE,
RECHTS: *Die »pompe-
janische« Ausmalung
des Salons stammt,
ebenso wie der Kristall-
Lüster, aus dem Jahr
1800. Die Vitrine ent-
hält eine Sammlung
alter Fächer.*
RECHTS: *Der Kachel-
ofen stammt aus der
Zeit Gustavs IV., lehnt
sich aber stilistisch an
eine frühere Epoche an:
Er wurde offensichtlich
um 1800 gebaut.*

DOUBLE PAGE
PRÉCÉDENTE, À
GAUCHE: *le lac de
Mälaren vu du perron.*
DOUBLE PAGE PRÉ-
CÉDENTE, À DROITE:
*Le décor «à la pom-
péienne» du salon date
de 1800, ainsi que le
lustre en cristal. Dans la
vitrine, une collection
d'éventails anciens.*
À DROITE: *Le poêle en
faïence date du règne
de Gustav IV mais il
emprunte son langage
stylistique à une période
antérieure et fut, de toute évidence, construit
vers 1800.*

S VARTSJÖ SLOTT

Mälaren

Carl Hårleman (1700–1753) was clearly one of the most brilliant architects of his time and it is hard to believe that his innovative talent has been neglected for so long. A son of the King's gardener who was orphaned at the age of seven, the young man won a financial grant through the influence of the famous architect Nicodemus Tessin. This enabled him to study fine arts in the Low Countries and Italy. But it was Paris, where he obtained the prestigious Premier Prix, that influenced him most strongly in his later work. In 1725, France was preparing to flood the civilised world with ornate *rocaille;* fortunately Hårleman, on his return to Sweden to supervise the decoration of the royal palace in Stockholm, had the wisdom to strip rococo of its superfluous elements and give it a Nordic flavour. The manor of Svartsjö, built in 1734, perfectly reflects the architectural vocabulary of Hårleman, notably in its pure lines, its great hall decorated with *trompe-l'œil* windows and *faux-marbre,* and its austere salons floored in pale wood. Recently saved from rack and ruin by the Statensfastighetsverk and temporarily decorated with 18th century furniture, paintings and fabrics, Svartsjö is a tribute to the talent of one of Sweden's greatest architects.

All the elegance of 18th-century Sweden is reflected in this wall surface, which is decorated with a blue and white floral fabric and a portrait of Queen Lovisa Ulrike.

In diesem mit einem blauweißen Blumenmusterstoff tapezierten Stück Wand, das ein Portrait der Königin Lovisa Ulrike ziert, spiegelt sich die ganze Eleganz des schwedischen 18. Jahrhunderts.

Toute l'élégance du 18ᵉ siècle suédois se reflète dans ce pan de mur tapissé d'un tissu floral bleu et blanc et sur lequel on a accroché le portrait de la reine Lovisa Ulrike.

Carl Hårleman (1700–1753) war einer der bedeutendsten
Architekten seiner Zeit und es ist eigentlich verwunderlich,
dass sein innovatives Talent so lange im Dunkeln geblieben ist.
Der früh verwaiste Sohn des Königlichen Gärtners erhielt auf
Fürsprache des berühmten Architekten Nicodemus Tessin ein
Stipendium, das es ihm ermöglichte, in den Niederlanden, Italien und Frankreich Kunst und Architektur zu studieren. Die
nachhaltigsten Einflüsse erfuhr er jedoch in Paris, wo er auch
den Premier Prix verliehen bekam. 1725 schickte Frankreich
sich an, die zivilisierte Welt mit den verschnörkelten Formen
des »Rocaille«-Stils zu überziehen. Hårleman, der nach Schweden zurückgekehrt war, um für die Ausgestaltung des Stockholmer Königspalasts zu sorgen, verstand es indes, dem Ro-
koko eine nordische Ausprägung zu geben. Inbild seiner
Formensprache ist das 1734 erbaute Schloss Svartsjö mit seinen
klaren Linien, seiner Ausschmückung des Großen Saals durch
Fenster in Trompe-l'Œil-Manier und Marmorimitat und seinen streng gehaltenen Salons mit hellen Holzfußböden. Dass
Svartsjö unlängst vor dem Verfall bewahrt und – zeitweilig –
mit Möbeln, Gemälden und Stoffen aus dem 18. Jahrhundert
versehen wurde, ist eine letzte Verbeugung vor Hårleman.

*The balanced rhythm in
its classical façade and
the spare elegance of its
ornamentation betray
the influence of 18th-
century France.*

*Der ausgewogene
Rhythmus der klassi-
schen Fassade und die
Eleganz des sparsam
eingesetzten Ornaments
verraten den Einfluss
der zeitgenössischen
französischen Archi-
tektur.*

*Le rythme équilibré de
sa façade classique et
l'élégance de ses rares
ornements trahissent
l'influence de l'archi-
tecture du 18ᵉ siècle
français.*

*The magnificent castle
of Svartsjö, seen from
the garden.*

*Blick vom Garten auf
das wunderschöne
Schloss Svartsjö.*

*Le magnifique château
de Svartsjö vu du jar-
din.*

Carl Hårleman (1700–1753) fut l'un des architectes les plus
brillants de son époque et on s'étonne de voir que son talent
innovateur est si longtemps resté dans l'obscurité. Fils du jardi-
nier du roi et orphelin à sept ans, le jeune homme obtint une
bourse grâce au célèbre architecte Nicodème II Tessin. Il put
ainsi étudier les beaux-arts aux Pays-Bas, en Italie et en France.
C'est à Paris, où il obtint le prestigieux Premier Prix, qu'il subit
la plus grande influence. En 1725, la France se préparait à inon-
der le monde civilisé des formes tarabiscotées du style rocaille,
mais Hårleman, de retour en Suède pour veiller à la décoration
du Palais Royal à Stockholm, sut dépouiller le «rococo» de ses
éléments superflus et lui donner un caractère nordique. Le
manoir de Svartsjö, bâti en 1734, reflète parfaitement le voca-
bulaire architectural de Hårleman, en témoignent ses lignes
épurées, son grand hall orné de fenêtres en trompe-l'œil et de
faux marbre et ses salons sévères dotés de sobres planchers en
bois clair. Sauvé récemment de la ruine par le Statensfastighetsverk et décoré – temporairement – avec des meubles, des
tableaux et des tissus 18ᵉ, Svartsjö rend hommage à l'un des
plus grands architectes du 18ᵉ siècle.

LEFT: *On the work-table, sketches by Hårleman and pieces of staff ornamentation reveal the architect's austerity as well as his respect for detail.*
FACING PAGE: *In one of Svartsjö's salons, a period table and chair strongly redolent of Hårleman. The plans, sketches and pieces of staff complete the illusion.*

LINKS: *Hårlemans Skizzen und Gipsorna-mente auf dem Arbeits-tisch zeigen seine plane-rische Geradlinigkeit und Detailgenauigkeit.*
RECHTE SEITE: *Ein zeitgenössisches Ensem-ble von Arbeitstisch und Stuhl beschwört in einem der Räume des Schlosses die Gestalt des Architekten herauf. Plä-ne, Skizzen und Gips-ornamente machen die Illusion perfekt.*

A GAUCHE: *Sur la table de travail, des cro-quis de Hårleman et des ornements en staff nous révèlent son souci de sobriété et son respect du détail.*
PAGE DE DROITE: *Dans un salon de Svartsjö, une table et une chaise d'époque évo-quent l'architecte. Les plans, les croquis et des fragments en staff com-plètent l'illusion.*

The main entrance hall,
known as the salon ital-
ien. Here Hårleman
showed that he could
create grandiose inter-
iors while economising
on architectural details
and avoiding all super-
fluous ornamentation.
The bust represents King
Frederik I.

In der großen Eingangs-
halle, dem so genannten
»italienischen Salon«,
bewies Hårleman, dass
er bei sparsamer Ver-
wendung von Baude-
tails und unter Verzicht
auf jedes überflüssige
Ornament grandiose
Innenräume zu schaffen
verstand. Die Büste
stellt König Frederik I.
dar.

Dans le grand hall d'en-
trée dit le «Salon ita-
lien», Hårleman a
prouvé qu'il pouvait
créer des intérieurs
grandioses en écono-
misant sur les détails
architecturaux et en
renonçant à tout orne-
ment superflu. Le buste
représente le roi Frede-
rik Ier.

ℳ ALMSTENHUSET

Uppland

Little known abroad but venerated in Sweden, the designer Carl Malmsten (1888–1972) is viewed as a major creative talent of the 20th century. He was born into a well-to-do Stockholm family; his father was a doctor and his maternal grandfather built the capital's Grand Hotel. As a young man Malmsten was strongly affected by his parents' divorce, turning to design as a consolation. It was he who created the furniture for the new city hall (Rådhuset) in 1912, and his style, based as it was on the principles of 18th-century cabinetmakers, was highly successful thereafter. He eventually married Siv Munthe, a young Norwegian of Flemish origin, and went to live at Solna in a Biedermeier wooden villa that King Oskar I had originally built for his mistress, Emilie Högqvist. In this modest house Malmsten was able to bring his most advanced ideas to fruition. His son Egil, who now runs Malmstenhuset and makes sure that its unique collection of furniture, lamps, carpets, fabrics and paintings stays together, remembers Malmsten as a passionate artist who hated cold functionalism and treated his creations like living people. Carl Malmsten died of a heart attack a few weeks after learning that there had been a fire in one of the rooms of his Solna residence.

In front of the house, a table and benches stand in the sunshine.

Vor dem Haus laden Tisch und Bänke dazu ein, sich in die Sonne zu setzen.

Devant la maison, une table et des bancs invitent à s'asseoir au soleil.

Der im Ausland kaum bekannte, doch in Schweden hochge-
achtete Designer Carl Malmsten (1888–1972) gilt als einer der
größten Innenraumgestalter des 20. Jahrhunderts. Malmsten
kam in Stockholm als Sohn einer wohlhabenden Familie zur
Welt. Schwer getroffen von der Scheidung seiner Eltern, such-
te der junge Mann Trost im Entwerfen. Er war es, der 1912 das
Mobiliar des neuen Stockholmer Rathauses, des Rådhuset,
gestaltete. Mit seinem Stil, der auf Prinzipien der Möbelbauer
des 18. Jahrhunderts fußte, errang er durchschlagenden Erfolg.
Malmsten heiratete Siv Munthe, eine junge Norwegerin flämi-
scher Herkunft, und ließ sich in Solna in einer biedermeier-
lichen Holzvilla nieder, die König Oskar I. für seine Maitresse
Emilie Högqvist hatte errichten lassen. Hier sollte Malmsten
seine fortschrittlichsten Ideen verwirklichen. Sein Sohn Egil
verwaltet das Malmstenhuset und kümmert sich um die Erhaltung dieses einmaligen Ensembles von Möbeln, Lampen, Teppichen, Stoffen und Gemälden. Er liebt es, die Erinnerung an
den passionierten Künstler wachzurufen, der kalten Funktio-
nalismus verabscheute und ein paar Wochen, nachdem er
erfahren hatte, dass in einem der Räume in seinem Haus in
Solna ein Feuer ausgebrochen war, einem Schlaganfall erlag.

*Built for Oskar I's mis-
tress, Malmstenhuset
reflects the sobriety of
the Biedermeier style.*

*Erbaut für die Geliebte
Oskars I., spiegelt
Malmstenhuset die
schnörkellose Architek-
tur des Biedermeier.*

*Construite pour la maî-
tresse d'Oskar Iᵉʳ, la
Malmstenhuset reflète
l'architecture sobre du
Biedermeier.*

Peu connu à l'étranger et vénéré en Suède, le designer Carl
Malmsten (1888–1972) est considéré comme l'un des plus
grands créateurs du 20ᵉ siècle. Né à Stockholm dans une famille aisée (son père était médecin et son grand-père maternel
avait bâti le célèbre Grand Hôtel dans la capitale), le jeune
homme très affecté par le divorce de ses parents, chercha
consolation dans le dessin. Ce fut lui qui conçut le mobilier
du nouvel Hôtel de Ville de Stockholm, le Rådhuset en 1912,
et son style, basé sur les principes des ébénistes du 18ᵉ siècle,
lui valut un succès retentissant. Malmsten épousa Siv Munthe,
une jeune Norvégienne d'origine flamande et s'installa à Solna
dans une villa en bois de style Biedermeier que le roi Oskar Iᵉʳ
avait fait construire pour sa maîtresse, Emilie Högqvist. C'est
dans cette modeste demeure qu'il allait réaliser ses idées les plus
avancées. Son fils Egil, qui gère le Malmstenhuset et s'efforce
de préserver cet ensemble unique de meubles, de lampes, de
tapis, de tissus et de tableaux, adore évoquer le souvenir de cet
artiste passionné qui détestait le fonctionnalisme froid, abor-
dait ses créations comme des êtres humains et mourut d'une
attaque, quelques semaines après avoir appris que sa maison
de Solna avait été la proie des flammes.

*Egil and his companion
Wiveca have kept the
kitchen exactly as it was
in Malmsten's time.*

*Egil und seine Lebens-
gefährtin Wiveca haben
die Küche nicht verän-
dert.*

*Egil et Wiveca – sa com-
pagne – n'ont pas touché
à la cuisine.*

LEFT: *This door lintel was designed by Malmsten, as were the chair and the small table.*

LINKS: *Den Türrahmen hat Malmsten entworfen. Auch der Stuhl und der kleine Tisch tragen seine Handschrift.*

A GAUCHE: *Le chambranle de la porte a été dessiné par Malmsten. La chaise et la petite table portent également sa signature.*

FACING PAGE: *Carl's furniture and Egil's watercolours remain in situ in the bedroom. The lampshades were made by Siv Munthe, using paper and dried leaves.*
RIGHT: *It was Malmsten himself who decided to decorate all the doors with borders and fillets in his favourite colours – these are in the passageway leading to the kitchen.*

LINKE SEITE: *Im Schlafzimmer findet man Carl Malmstens Möbel und die Aquarelle von Egil. Die mit getrockneten Blättern verzierten Papierlampenschirme hat Siv Munthe gefertigt.*
RECHTS: *Es war Malmsten, der beschloss, alle Türen mit Leisten und Reliefelementen in seinen Lieblingsfarben zu schmücken, so die Flurtür zur Küche.*

PAGE DE GAUCHE: *Dans la chambre à coucher, on découvre les meubles de Carl Malmsten et les aquarelles d'Egil. Les abat-jour en papier décorés de feuilles séchées sont l'œuvre de Siv Munthe.*

A DROITE: *C'est Malmsten qui décida de décorer toutes les portes avec des filets et des rechampis exécutés dans ses couleurs favorites. En témoignent celles du couloir qui mène à la cuisine.*

FACING PAGE: *One of the bedrooms overlooking the garden was converted into a study-cum-studio. The furniture is by Malmsten and the tiled stove dates from the early 20th century.*
RIGHT: *The kitchen retains its original Malmsten paintwork and old-fashioned pots and pans.*

LINKE SEITE: *Eines der Zimmer, die sich zum Garten hin öffnen, wurde zum Büro- und Atelierraum umfunktioniert. Das Mobiliar entwarf Malmsten. Der Kachelofen stammt vom Anfang des 20. Jahrhunderts.*
RECHTS: *In der Küche sind die Original-»Malmsten«-Farben und das alte Kochgeschirr erhalten geblieben.*

PAGE DE GAUCHE: *Une des chambres qui donnent sur le jardin a été transformée en bureau-atelier. Le mobilier est de Malmsten et le poêle en faïence date du début du 20ᵉ siècle.*
A DROITE: *La cuisine a gardé ses couleurs «Malmsten» d'origine et sa batterie de cuisine ancienne.*

HAGAPAVILJONGEN
Gustav III
Uppland

In 1787, King Gustav III of Sweden commissioned the architect Olof Tempelman to build a pavilion at Haga on the site of the already existing manor of Brahelund near Stockholm. Heavily influenced as he was by his travels in France and Italy, the King was obsessed with the idea of recreating a Swedish Petit Trianon, where he could relax far away from the court and its political intrigues. He employed the greatest contemporary decorators in Europe, Jean-Baptiste and Louis Masreliez; also the cabinetmakers Erik Öhrmark, Georg Haupt and Gustaf Adolf Ditzinger, and the caster and engraver Fredrik Ludwig Rung. Today the pavilion at Haga is unusual among royal residences, in that few follies erected by a sovereign have ever attained such a degree of perfection. A blend of extreme elegance and sobriety, Haga was filled with Pompeiian décor, neo-classical furniture, fine tiled stoves and glittering chandeliers. On 16 March 1792, in the evening, the King left Haga to attend the Opera in Stockholm. There he died, at the hands of the assassin Jacob Johan Anckarström, and an entire era died with him.

PREVIOUS PAGES: *From the far side of the water, Olof Tempelman's architectural vision is shown to great advantage.*
LEFT: *an à l'antique decorative detail on one of the panels in the antechamber.*

VORHERGEHENDE DOPPELSEITE: *Vom gegenüber liegenden Ufer hat man eine sehr schöne Sicht auf die von Olof Tempelman entworfene elegante Architektur.*
LINKS: *ein Detail des antikisierenden Dekors auf einer der Tafeln im Vorzimmer.*

DOUBLE PAGE PRÉCÉDENTE: *De l'autre côté de la rive, on a une très belle vue sur l'architecture élégante imaginée par Olof Tempelman.*
A GAUCHE: *un détail du décor à l'antique sur un des panneaux de l'antichambre.*

1787 beauftragte König Gustav III. den Architekten Olof Tempelman mit dem Bau eines Schlösschens in Haga nahe Stockholm, wo sich bereits das Anwesen Brahelund befand. Beein-
flusst von seinen Reisen nach Frankreich und Italien, wollte
der König ein schwedisches Petit Trianon errichten, wo er vom
Hof und den dortigen politischen Intrigen Abstand gewinnen
und sich erholen konnte. Um diesem Traum in Stein den letzten Schliff zu geben, wandte er sich an die größten Innenarchi-
tekten seiner Zeit, Jean-Baptiste und Louis Masreliez, an die
Möbelbauer Erik Öhrmark, Georg Haupt und Gustaf Adolf
Ditzinger sowie an den Gießer und Ziselierer Fredrik Ludwig
Rung. Selten hat ein von einem Herrscher erbautes Lustschloss
derartige Vollkommenheit erreicht. In seiner Verbindung von
Eleganz und Nüchternheit hat das Bauwerk, das pompejani-
sche Dekorationen, klassizistisches Mobiliar, Kachelöfen und
prächtig glitzernde Kristall-Lüster unter einem Dach vereint,
über die Zeiten hinweg nichts von seinem Reiz verloren. Von
Haga aus machte sich der König am Abend des 16. März 1792
auf den Weg zu seiner Loge in der Stockholmer Oper, wo der
Attentäter Jacob Johan Anckarström seinem Leben – und
damit einer ganzen Epoche – ein Ende setzte.

En 1787, le roi Gustav III demanda à l'architecte Olof Tempelman de construire un pavillon à Haga, à une distance
agréable de Stockholm, sur un site où se trouvait déjà le
manoir de Brahelund. Très influencé par ses voyages en France
et en Italie, le roi était obsédé par l'idée de créer un Petit Trianon suédois où il pourrait se reposer, loin de la Cour et des
intrigues politiques. Pour réaliser ce rêve de pierre, il s'adressa
aux plus grands décorateurs de l'époque, Jean-Baptiste et Louis
Masreliez, aux ébénistes Erik Öhrmark, Georg Haupt et Gustaf Adolf Ditzinger et au «fondeur-ciseleur» Fredrik Ludwig
Rung. Le pavillon de Haga occupe une place tout à fait particulière parmi les résidences royales, car une «folie» érigée par
un souverain a rarement atteint un tel degré de perfection.
Alliant l'élégance à la sobriété et réunissant sous le même toit
des décorations pompéiennes, un mobilier néoclassique, des
poêles en faïence et des chandeliers ruisselants de cristal, Haga
n'a pas cessé d'exercer son charme intemporel. Le 16 mars
1792 au soir, le roi quitta Haga pour sa loge de l'Opéra de
Stockholm et c'est là qu'il mourut, assassiné par Jacob Johan
Anckarström … et toute une époque avec lui.

ABOVE: *In the dining room, the frescoes, the buffet tables designed by Desprez and made by Pehr Ljung in 1791, and the marbles of Apollo and Vesta, all evoke the theme of Antiquity.*

OBEN: *Die Fresken, die von Desprez entworfenen und 1791 von Pehr Ljung ausgeführten Tische zum Anrichten wie auch die Marmorfiguren von Apollo und Vesta beschwören im Speisesaal die Antike.*

CI-DESSUS: *Dans la salle à manger, les fresques, les tables-buffets dessinées par Desprez et exécutées en 1791 par Pehr Ljung et les marbres représentant Apollon et Vesta évoquent l'Antiquité.*

FACING PAGE: *In the Mirror Salon, a "klismos" chair by Erik Öhrmark goes very well with the gilded panels by Pehr Ljung and Jean-Baptiste Masreliez.*

RECHTE SEITE: *Erik Öhrmarks »Klismos«-Stuhl im Spiegelsalon harmoniert perfekt mit den vergoldeten Täfelungen von Pehr Ljung und Jean-Baptiste Masreliez.*

PAGE DE DROITE: *Dans le Salon des Miroirs, une chaise «klismos» signée Erik Öhrmark s'harmonise parfaitement avec les lambris sculptés et dorés par Pehr Ljung et Jean-Baptiste Masreliez.*

LEFT: *The walls of the King's bedroom, like the alcove bed and the furniture, is covered with precious Lyon silk. In 1792, Gustav's future assassin came here to peer at him through one of the windows.*
FACING PAGE: *A detail of the chaise longue, created by Öhrmark in 1792; it was originally covered in striped blue silk.*

LINKS: *Im Schlafgemach des Königs sind Wände, Alkovenbett und Mobiliar mit wunderschöner Lyoner Seide bezogen. 1792 wurde Gustav III. hier von seinem späteren Mörder durch ein Fenster bespäht.*
RECHTE SEITE: *Detail der 1790 von Öhrmark entworfenen Chaiselongue, die ursprünglich mit blaugestreifter Seide bezogen war.*

A GAUCHE: *Dans la chambre à coucher du roi, les murs, le lit d'alcôve et le mobilier sont recouverts d'une magnifique soie de Lyon. En 1792, le futur assassin de Gustav III était venu le contempler par l'une des fenêtres.*
PAGE DE DROITE: *détail de la chaise longue, créée en 1790 par Öhrmark et qui était recouverte à l'origine d'une soie rayée bleue.*

MARTINE COLLIANDER

Stockholm

Martine Colliander is very partial to white, so partial indeed that
she views it as synonymous with purity and simplicity. Apart from a
single, brightly-coloured flower, a family photograph taken on the
island where she grew up, and the marmalade coat of her splendid
tomcat, Stene, she will allow no other hue anywhere near her. Yet
white is not her only passion; she also loves fabrics, drapes and
Gustavian furniture (on condition, obviously, that they are of her
favourite non-colour). After deeply regretting the sale of her farmhouse beside a lake, she decided to replace it – literally – with the
top floor of a 1900's building in Stockholm, thus proving to her crit-
ics that you really can create an airy, charming, country atmosphere
in the middle of town. It is now several years since this fair, frail
Swedish woman started a business copying Gustavian furniture,
embroidered fabrics and household linen. So it was a breeze for her
to transform her fifth-floor "stuga" into an immaculate farmhouse,
white and austere, to which the curve of an 18th-century chair and a
table with a skirt of embroidered linen add a note of entirely femi-
nine elegance.

*Detail of an embroi-
dered voile curtain,
made to a design by
Martine Colliander.*

*Detail eines bestickten
Voile-Vorhangs nach
einem Entwurf von
Martine Colliander.*

*Détail d'un rideau en
voile brodé, d'après un
dessin de Martine Col-
liander.*

Martine Colliander liebt Weiß, das für sie gleichbedeutend ist mit Reinheit und Einfachheit. Der Farbtupfer einer Blüte, das Foto ihrer Familie, aufgenommen auf der Insel des Archipels, wo sie aufwuchs, oder das getigerte Fellkleid ihres prächtigen Katers Stene sind Ausnahmen: Ansonsten duldet sie in ihrer unmittelbaren Umgebung keine Farben. Doch Weiß ist nicht die einzige Vorliebe Martines, die ebenso viel für Stoffe, Vorhänge und Möbel im gustavianischen Stil übrig hat – vorausgesetzt natürlich, diese haben ihre Lieblings-Nichtfarbe. Weil sie es sehr bedauerte, ihren Bauernhof an einem See verkauft zu haben und sie sich in das obere Geschoss eines Gebäudes der Jahrhundertwende im Herzen von Stockholm verliebte, beschloss sie, ihren Gegnern zu beweisen, dass sich auch unter dem Dach eines Stadthauses ein lichtdurchflutetes Landhaus voller Anmut herrichten lässt. Seit einigen Jahren schon kümmert sich die zierliche blonde Schwedin um die Neuauflage von Möbeln im gustavianischen Stil, um bestickte Stoffe und Hauswäsche. Deshalb gelang es ihr im Handumdrehen, ihre städtische »stuga« im fünften Stock in ein Landhaus zu verwandeln, wie es weißer und schlichter nicht sein könnte.

Martine Colliander adore le blanc, pour elle cette teinte est synonyme de pureté et de simplicité. Et mis à part la tache plus vive d'une fleur, d'une photo de sa famille prise dans une île de l'archipel (celle où elle a grandi) ou la robe tigrée de son magnifique matou Stene, elle n'admet aucune couleur dans son environnement immédiat. Mais le blanc n'est pas le seul amour de Martine qui adore aussi les tissus, les voilages et les meubles gustaviens (à condition évidemment qu'ils aient sa non-couleur favorite). Comme elle a beaucoup regretté d'avoir vendu sa ferme près d'un lac et qu'elle s'est éprise de la partie supérieure d'un immeuble 1900 au cœur de Stockholm, elle a décidé de prouver à ses adversaires que l'on peut facilement créer une maison de campagne lumineuse et pleine de charme sous le toit d'une maison citadine. Voilà quelques années déjà que la blonde et frêle Suédoise s'occupe de la réédition des meubles gustaviens, de tissus brodés et de linge de maison. Il ne lui a donc guère fallu qu'un tour de main pour transformer sa «stuga» au cinquième étage en ville en une ferme immaculée, blanche et sobre à souhait où le galbe d'une chaise 18e et une table juponnée de lin brodé ajoutent une note d'élégance féminine.

LEFT: *The adobe fire-place in Martine's bed-room, copied from an antique original. The big linen cupboard was specially designed by her.*
FACING PAGE: *When she knocked down some partitions the new owner discovered this extraordinary brick construction.*
FOLLOWING PAGES: *Stene the cat, constantly on the watch. Martine, for once abandoning her insistence on white, has painted the interior of this cupboard a vivid lavender blue.*

LINKS: *Der Adobe-Kamin in Martines Zimmer ist einem historischen Vorbild nach-empfunden. Der große Wäscheschrank trägt ebenfalls ihre Hand-schrift.*
RECHTE SEITE: *Beim Einreißen der Zwi-schenwände entdeckte die neue Eigentümerin eine auffällige Back-steinkonstruktion.*
FOLGENDE DOPPEL-SEITE: *Stene scheint stets auf der Lauer. Von ihrer Lieblingsfarbe Weiß abweichend, hat Martine das Schrank-innere in Lavendelblau gestrichen.*

A GAUCHE: *Dans la chambre de Martine, une cheminée en «ado-le» copiée sur un modè-le ancien. La grande armoire à linge porte également sa griffe.*
PAGE DE DROITE: *En abattant des cloisons, la nouvelle propriétaire a découvert une extraordi-naire construction en briques.*
DOUBLE PAGE SUI-VANTE: *Stene semble toujours aux aguets. Martine, délaissant son blanc favori, a peint l'intérieur de l'armoire en bleu lavande.*

Martine Colliander has
brilliantly succeeded
in creating a country
atmosphere on the fifth
floor of a 19th-century
building in the middle
of Stockholm. Her mag-
nificent brick floor con-
tributes mightily to the
illusion.

Martine Colliander ist
das Kunststück gelun-
gen, im fünften Stock
eines Jahrhundertwen-
degebäudes mitten in
Stockholm eine länd-
liche Atmosphäre zu
schaffen. Ein wunder-
schöner Steinboden
macht die Illusion
perfekt.

Martine Colliander a
parfaitement réussi à
créer une ambiance
campagnarde au cin-
quième étage d'un
immeuble 1900 en plein
cœur de Stockholm. Le
magnifique sol en pierre
contribue à l'illusion.

ABOVE: *The kitchen, naturally, is immaculately white. Even Martine's favourite dishes tend to be white: fresh pasta, rice.*
RIGHT: *The designer works under the slope of her roof, close to a skylight.*
FACING PAGE: *Martine has draped the beams near her bed with diaphanous embroidered curtains.*
FOLLOWING PAGES: *Martine is a master of the subtle play of tones within her chosen palette of non-colour.*

OBEN: *Die Küche ist selbstverständlich weiß. Sogar Martines Lieblingsspeisen – frische Nudeln und Reis – verraten ihre Vorliebe.*
RECHTS: *der Arbeitsplatz der Designerin unter einem Dachfenster.*
RECHTE SEITE: *Martine hat die Balken in der Nähe ihres Bettes mit durchscheinenden, bestickten Vorhängen drapiert.*
FOLGENDE DOPPELSEITE: *Martines fantastische Ton-in-Ton-Kompositionen verraten viel Fingerspitzengefühl.*

CI-DESSUS: *La cuisine est bien sûr immaculée. Même les plats préférés de Colliander, pâtes fraîches et riz, trahissent son penchant pour la non-couleur.*
A DROITE: *La créatrice travaille sous le toit en pente, près d'une lucarne.*
PAGE DE DROITE: *Martine a drapé les poutres près de son lit de rideaux diaphanes brodés.*
DOUBLE PAGE SUIVANTE: *Martine joue subtilement avec sa palette monochrome et ses compositions ton sur ton nous émerveillent.*

$\mathcal{H}$AZELIUSHUSET

Stockholm

The Skansen open air museum is now a part of the fascinating "Sweden in Miniature" exhibition on the island of Djurgården. Skansen was the first museum of its kind in the country; its site is also the birthplace of the schoolteacher Artur Hazelius, who founded the "village" in 1891. The oldest part of Hazeliushuset consists of a country house built at the beginning of the 18th century for Count Carl Frölich. After serving as a studio for the weaver Isac Fritz, the house was heavily altered and rented in 1831 to J. A. Hazelius, a future general. He was the father of the celebrated founder of Skansen – and of the Nordiska Museet in Stockholm. The earlier sections of the building reflect the comfortable, bourgeois taste that predominated during the reign of Carl Johan (1810–1844); this was the Swedish version of an aesthetic which might be placed midway between French Empire and German Biedermeier. But as soon as the visitor leaves the formal décor and plunges into the labyrinth of romantic rooms adjoining – which include Hazelius's own study, a charming kitchen full of bright pewter plates, and bedrooms complete with tiled stoves and four-poster beds – the Hazeliushuset begins to offer nostalgic glimpses of a more distant past.

A magnificent 18th-century gilt-bronze clock, made by the clockmaker Hans Wessman, hangs on the dining room wall.

Eine prächtige, aus dem 18. Jahrhundert stammende Pendeluhr aus vergoldeter Bronze von dem Uhrmacher Hans Wessman schmückt eine Wand des Esszimmers.

Une somptueuse pendule 18ᵉ en bronze doré – œuvre de l'horloger Hans Wessman – orne un mur de la salle à manger.

Das Freilichtmuseum Skansen, das erste Museum seiner Art, ist heute Teil eines faszinierenden »Schweden en miniature« mitten auf der Insel Djurgården. Hier kam der Lehrer Artur Hazelius zur Welt, der 1891 das »Dorf« Skansen gründete. Der älteste Teil von Hazeliushuset ist ein Anfang des 18. Jahrhunderts für den Grafen Carl Frölich errichtetes Landhaus. Nachdem es dem Weber Isac Fritz als Werkstatt gedient hatte, wurde es vollständig umgebaut und 1831 an den Hauptmann und späteren General J. A. Hazelius vermietet, dessen Sohn dann das berühmte Freilichtmuseum sowie das Nordiska Museet in Stockholm gründen sollte. Der vordere Teil des Gebäudes spiegelt den behäbigen bürgerlichen Stil, der unter der Regierung von Karl XIV. Johan (1810–1844) den Ton angab: die schwedische Version einer Ästhetik zwischen französischem Empire und deutschem Biedermeier. Doch sobald der Besucher aus diesem förmlichen Rahmen in ein Gewirr romantisch anmutender Räumlichkeiten gelangt – das Arbeitszimmer von Hazelius, eine blitzblanke Küche, in der die Zinnteller schimmern, Schlafkammern, die mit Himmelbetten und Kachelöfen ausgestattet sind –, bietet das Hazeliushuset einen Ausflug in eine nostalgische Vergangenheit.

An egg-yolk yellow façade and pistachio green shutters: bright colours, beloved of the 18th century.

Dottergelbe Fassade und pistaziengrüne Fensterläden: Im 18. Jahrhundert waren lebhafte Farben beliebt.

Façade jaune d'œuf et volets pistache: on aimait les couleurs vives au 18ᵉ siècle.

Le musée en plein air de Skansen fait aujourd'hui partie de cette fascinante «Suède en miniature» au cœur de l'île de Djurgården. Il fut le premier musée du genre et vit naître l'instituteur Artur Hazelius qui fonda le «village» de Skansen en 1891. La plus ancienne partie de la Hazeliushuset est composée d'une maison de campagne construite au début du 18ᵉ siècle, pour le comte Carl Frölich. Après avoir servi d'atelier au tisserand Isac Fritz, la demeure subit des transformations importantes et fut louée en 1831 au capitaine et futur général J. A. Hazelius, le père du fondateur du célèbre musée en plein air et du Nordiska Museet à Stockholm. La partie antérieure de la maison reflète le goût cossu et bourgeois dominant sous le règne de Carl Johan (1810–1844), la version suédoise d'une esthétique à mi-chemin entre le style Empire français et le Biedermeier allemand. Mais dès que le visiteur quitte ce décor formel pour un dédale de pièces à l'ambiance romantique – le bureau de Hazelius, une cuisine pimpante où luisent des assiettes en étain et des chambres à coucher dotées de lits à baldaquin et de poêles en faïence –, le Hazeliushuset offre une promenade à travers un passé délicieusement nostalgique.

A Victorian chair, its seat covered in white cotton with frivolous flounces.

Die Sitzflächen der viktorianischen Stühle verschwinden unter einem mit neckischen Volants verzierten Baumwollbezug.

L'assise des chaises victoriennes disparaît sous une housse en coton blanc garnie de volants frivoles.

FACING PAGE:
Scoured floorboards, rustic furniture and white cotton curtains – newly washed, starched and ironed. Everything here is in keeping with the fresh, clean image of the Swedish kitchen.
RIGHT: *In the library, the furniture is comfortably bourgeois, while the oil lamp, table cover and lace curtains reflect the cumbersome taste of the Victorian era.*

LINKE SEITE: *Blank-gescheuerte Dielen, rustikale Möbel und frisch gewaschene, gestärkte und gebügelte Vorhänge »nach Hausfrauenart«: Nicht umsonst hat die schwedische Küche den Ruf, hell und reinlich zu sein.*
RECHTS: *In der Bibliothek spiegeln wuchtige bürgerliche Möbel, Petroleumlampe, Tischteppich und Spitzenvorhänge den etwas behäbigen Geschmack der Bewohner im viktorianischen Zeitalter.*

PAGE DE GAUCHE: *Planchers récurés, meubles rustiques et rideaux «bonne femme» en coton blanc fraîchement lavés, amidonnés et repassés: la réputation de la cuisine suédoise propre et claire n'est plus à faire.*
A DROITE: *Dans la bibliothèque, le mobilier bourgeois et cossu, la lampe à pétrole, le tapis de table et les rideaux en dentelle reflètent le goût un peu lourd des habitants de l'époque victorienne.*

FACING PAGE: *The bedroom floor is decorated with stencils.*
ABOVE: *The antechamber reflects the rigidity of the Carl Johan period, the general effect being one of precision and order.*
RIGHT: *a small cradle with period curtains, next to a tiled stove.*
FOLLOWING PAGES: *The painted, rustic furniture, stencilled floorboards and walls covered in amateur faux-marbre reflect the gentle sobriety of the Gustavian style.*

LINKE SEITE: *Der Boden des Schlafzimmers wurde in Schablonentechnik bemalt.*
OBEN: *Im Vorzimmer zeichnet sich die Strenge des Zeitalters Karl XIV. Johans ab. Die Ausstattung lässt die Neigung zu Ordnung und Klarheit erkennen.*
RECHTS: *eine Wiege mit Vorhängen aus damaliger Zeit, daneben der Kachelofen.*
FOLGENDE DOPPEL-SEITE: *Das bemalte rustikale Mobiliar, die Dielen und die marmorierten Wände zeigen die Schlichtheit des gustavianischen Stils.*

PAGE DE GAUCHE: *Le sol de la chambre est décoré au pochoir.*
CI-DESSUS: *L'antichambre reflète la rigidité de l'époque Carl-Johan et l'ensemble trahit un penchant pour l'ordre et la netteté.*
A DROITE: *un berceau à petits rideaux d'époque près d'un poêle en faïence.*
DOUBLE PAGE SUI-VANTE: *Le mobilier rustique peint, les planchers décorés au pochoir et les murs recouverts d'un faux marbre d'amateur reflètent la sobriété du style gustavien.*

SKOGAHOLM HERRGÅRD

Stockholm

The original manor of Skogaholm was at Närke, in the parish of Svennevad, and what is now the main part of the building was a piece of the Skogaholm Bruk Manufacturing Company. Later, Skogaholm was dismantled and reassembled in the middle of the open air museum at Skansen. Ever since its arrival, this magnificent 1680s construction has been an inspiration to Swedes, many of whom cite the pretty ochre-painted manor as their dream house. All the same, admirers of the "herrgård" are not usually aware that this elegant ensemble is no more than a skilfully crafted hotchpotch of various buildings brought from the provinces of Närke, Småland and Östergötland. Nor do they realise that the original façade of the main house was painted a traditional red and that the windows were enlarged at the end of the 18th-century. What really matters is that Skogaholm displays to its thousands of visitors a range of elegant interiors in which the Gustavian style predominates. At the same time the portraits of former inmates, the decorated panelling, the "baron's study" and the "baroness's bedroom" reflect the tastes and customs of an intriguing period.

The "Baron" pokes the logs in his drawing room fireplace.

Der »Baron« schürt das Feuer im Kamin des Salons.

Le «baron» attise le feu dans la cheminée du salon.

Ursprünglich lag das Gutshaus Skogaholm in Närke, im Kirchspiel Svennevad, und sein heutiger Hauptbau gehörte zur Manufaktur Skogaholm Bruk. Später wurde Skogaholm an Ort und Stelle zerlegt und im Freilichtmuseum Skansen wieder zusammengebaut. Seitdem ist dieser herrliche Bau aus den 1680er Jahren für die Schweden ein ständiger Quell der Inspiration gewesen: Das bildhübsche ockerfarbene Landschloss mit seinem bemerkenswerten Dach schwebt ihnen oft als ihr Traumhaus vor. Und doch ist den Bewunderern des »herrgård« vielfach nicht bekannt, dass das elegante Ensemble in Wirklichkeit nur eine geschickt zusammengetragene Musteranlage von Bauwerken aus Närke, Småland und Östergötland ist. Auch wissen sie oft nicht, dass die Fassade des Wohntrakts in traditionellem Rot gestrichen war und die Fenster Ende des 18. Jahrhunderts vergrößert worden sind. Gleichviel: Heute bietet Skogaholm seinen Besuchern eine Auswahl eleganter Interieurs, unter denen der gustavianische Stil den Ton angibt. Und die Portraits der einstigen Bewohner, der Wennerstedt, die verzierten Täfelungen, das »Kabinett des Barons« und das »Schlafzimmer der Baronin« zeigen die geschmacklichen Vorlieben und die Gebräuche einer faszinierenden Epoche.

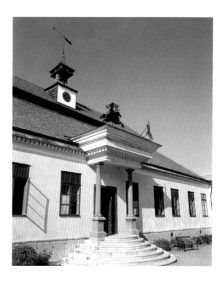

The main building at Skogaholm was once a part of the Skogaholm Bruk factory at Närke in the parish of Svennevad.

Der Wohntrakt von Skogaholm gehörte früher zur Manufaktur Skogaholm Bruk in Närke, Kirchspiel Svennevad.

Le corps de logis de Skogaholm faisait jadis partie de la Manufacture de Skogaholm Bruk, située dans la paroisse de Svennevad à Närke.

A l'origine, le manoir de Skogaholm se trouvait à Närke, dans la paroisse de Svennevad et ce qui en est aujourd'hui le bâtiment principal faisait partie de la Manufacture de Skogaholm Bruk. Skogaholm fut ensuite démonté sur place et rassemblé au cœur du musée en plein air de Skansen. Depuis, cette magnifique construction des années 1680 n'a jamais cessé d'inspirer les Suédois; d'ailleurs avec son remarquable toit à gradins, ce joli manoir couleur ocre jaune est souvent leur maison de rêves. En revanche, les admirateurs du «herrgård» ignorent souvent que cet ensemble élégant n'est en réalité qu'un échantillonnage astucieux composé de bâtiments provenant des provinces de Närke, Småland et Östergötland. Ils ne savent pas non plus qu'à l'origine, la façade du corps de logis était peinte en rouge traditionnel et que les fenêtres furent agrandies à la fin du 18e siècle. Peu importe, car de nos jours Skogaholm offre à ses milliers de visiteurs un choix d'intérieurs élégants où domine le style gustavien. Et les portraits des anciens habitants – les Wennerstedt –, les lambris décorés, le «cabinet du baron» et «la chambre à coucher de la baronne» reflètent les goûts et les coutumes d'une époque fascinante.

Benches in the hall, with its trompe l'œil décor, stone flags and beaten copper sconces.

Der mit Sitzbänken versehene Eingangsbereich wartet mit einem Trompe-l'Œil-Dekor, dicken Steinplatten und gehämmerten Kupferappliken auf.

L'entrée garnie de banquettes offre un décor en trompe-l'œil, de grosses dalles en pierre et des appliques en cuivre battu.

LEFT: *The Gustavian austerity of the former dining room is lightened by a splendid crystal chandelier.*
FACING PAGE: *raw linen covering a chair and fireguard in one of the salons.*

LINKS: *Die gustavianische Strenge des früheren Prunkspeisesaals wird durch den überreichen Glanz eines wunderschönen Kristall-Lüsters gemildert.*
RECHTE SEITE: *In dem nach pompejanischer Manier dekorierten Salon verschwinden die Stühle und der Ofenschirm unter Bezügen aus ungefärbter Leinwand.*

A GAUCHE: *La sévérité gustavienne de l'ancienne salle à manger d'apparat est adoucie par la présence exubérante d'un magnifique lustre en cristal.*
PAGE DE DROITE: *Dans un salon décoré à la pompéienne, les sièges et le pare-feu disparaissent sous des housses en toile écrue.*

RIGHT: *A plaster bust of King Gustav III surveys the sober décor of the "matsal".*

RECHTS: *Die Gipsbüste Gustavs III. beherrscht die nüchterne Einrichtung des »matsal«.*

A DROITE: *Le buste en plâtre du roi Gustav III domine le décor sobre de la «matsal».*

FACING PAGE: *the green half-light of the antechamber and bedroom, pierced by a ray of sunshine.*
ABOVE: *a magnificent four-poster in the bedroom, whose walls and ceiling are richly decorated.*
RIGHT: *a pewter plate and matching jug against a trompe-l'œil panel.*

LINKE SEITE: *Vorzimmer und Schlafzimmer sind in ein von grünen Reflexen durchsetztes Dämmerlicht getaucht, nur über eine Stelle der Wand streift ein Sonnenstrahl.*
OBEN: *Ein prächtiges Himmelbett beherrscht ein Schlafzimmer mit reich verzierter Täfelung und Decke.*
RECHTS: *Zinnteller und passende Wasserkanne heben sich von der Trompe-l'Œil-Täfelung ab.*

PAGE DE GAUCHE: *L'antichambre et la chambre à coucher baignent dans une pénombre à reflets verdâtres et un rayon de soleil hésitant caresse un pan de mur.*
CI-DESSUS: *Un somptueux lit à baldaquin domine une chambre à coucher dont les lambris et le plafond sont richement décorés.*
A DROITE: *Un plat en étain et l'aiguière assortie se détachent sur un lambris en trompe-l'œil.*

RIGHT: *Even in the richest houses, the bedrooms were remarkably simple. Here the baldachin is draped with white muslin.*

RECHTS: *Selbst in den prächtigsten Behausungen sind die Schlafzimmer ausgesprochen schlicht gehalten. Hier ist der Betthimmel mit weißem Musselin drapiert.*

A DROITE: *Même dans les demeures les plus somptueuses, les chambres à coucher sont d'une simplicité exemplaire. Ici le baldaquin a été drapé avec une étamine blanche.*

FAR LEFT: *A chambermaid dressed in period costume draws the striped cotton curtains.*
LEFT: *in the children's bedroom, beds of various sizes.*
FACING PAGE: *near the window in the small salon, a bobbin-frame for making lace.*

GANZ LINKS: *Eine Hausangestellte im zeitgenössischen Gewand arrangiert die Vorhänge aus gestreiftem Voile.*
LINKS: *In einem Kinderzimmer befinden sich maßgefertigte Betten.*

RECHTE SEITE: *In dem kleinen Salon steht nahe dem Fenster ein Klöppelkissen.*

A L'EXTRÊME GAUCHE: *Une servante en costume d'époque arrange les rideaux en voile rayé.*
A GAUCHE: *Dans une chambre d'enfant, des lits à la taille des différents occupants.*
PAGE DE DROITE: *Dans le petit salon, près de la fenêtre, un métier sur lequel on faisait une dentelle aux fuseaux.*

$\mathscr{K}$YRKHULTSSTUGAN

Stockholm

It has been some time since the Kyrkhultsstugan – the farm of Kyrkhult – was moved from its original site in the province of Blekinge to the open air museum of Skansen in southeast Sweden. This remarkable building would no longer be standing were it not for the perspicacity and initiative of Skansen's founder, Artur Hazelius, and the dedication of those who carry on the work that Hazelius liked to call the "archaeology of the past". Sited behind the church of Seglora, which was built in 1729 and comes from the province of Västergötland, this squat, low farmhouse gives the impression of being squeezed between two capacious barns. Nevertheless, while everything suggests that the "stuga" dates from the 18th-century, this type of building – whose central section is covered with a layer of grass – actually dates from the Middle Ages. Inside, Kyrkhultsstugan is very spacious and if you look closely at the big fireplace with its bread oven, the robust furniture, the tapestries and the mural decorations with their peasant motifs, you appreciate the true 'wealth' of its former inhabitants. In the bedroom, the perfect symmetry of a pair of alcove beds behind checked curtains evokes for us the romance of a vanished time.

LEFT: *The slatted facade of the farmhouse is an invitation to climbing plants.*
ABOVE: *The date of the building is carved on one wall of the hallway.*

LINKS: *Mit einem Lattengerüst versehen, begünstigt die Fassade des Bauernhauses das Wachstum von Kletterpflanzen.*
OBEN: *Das Baujahr ist in eine Wand des Eingangsbereichs geschnitzt.*

A GAUCHE: *La façade de la ferme, entièrement lattée, encourage les plantes grimpantes.*
CI-DESSUS: *La date de la construction est gravée dans une des parois de l'entrée.*

Schon vor langer Zeit wurde Kyrkhultsstugan, der ursprünglich in der Provinz Blekinge angesiedelte Bauernhof von Kyrkhult, nach Südostschweden ins Freilichtmuseum Skansen verlegt. Den Erhalt dieses außergewöhnlichen Bauwerks verdanken wir der Initiative und dem Weitblick des Museumsgründers Artur Hazelius sowie all jenen, die gegenwärtig seine Arbeit als »Archäologe der Vergangenheit« fortführen. Heute hinter der 1729 erbauten Kirche von Seglora aus der Provinz Västergötland gelegen, erweckt das stämmig-gedrungene Bauernhaus den Eindruck, als ducke es sich zwischen zwei hohe und weitläufige Scheunen. Auch wenn alles dafür zu sprechen scheint, dass die »stuga« aus dem 18. Jahrhundert stammt, so reicht dieser Gebäudetypus, dessen Hauptbau ein mit Gras bewachsenes Dach aufweist, bis ins Mittelalter zurück. Im Inneren erweist sich Kyrkhultsstugan als sehr geräumig, und wenn man sich die imposante Feuerstelle mit ihrem Brotofen, das robuste Mobiliar, die an den Wänden hängenden Tapisserien und Dekorationen mit ihren volkstümlichen Motiven von nahem anschaut, gewinnt man eine Vorstellung vom »Reichtum« der einstigen Bewohner. Die vollendete Symmetrie zweier mit Karovorhängen versehenen Alkovenbetten im Schlafzimmer versetzt uns zurück in die Stimmung einer fernen Zeit.

Kyrkhultsstugan is surrounded by a traditional fence of woven branches.

Kyrkhultsstugan ist umgeben von einer traditionellen Einfriedung aus Ästen.

Kyrkhultsstugan est entourée d'une clôture traditionnelle faite de branches.

Il y a longtemps déjà que la Kyrkhultsstugan – la ferme de Kyrkhult –, originaire de la province de Blekinge, a été transférée au sud-est de la Suède, au musée en plein air de Skansen. Et nous devons la sauvegarde de ce bâtiment exceptionnel à l'initiative et la perspicacité de son fondateur Artur Hazelius et à tous ceux qui perpétuent de nos jours son travail d'«archéologue du passé». Située aujourd'hui derrière l'église de Seglora, construite en 1729 et provenant de la province de Västergötland, la ferme trapue et basse donne l'impression d'être coincée entre deux granges vastes et hautes. Néanmoins, si tout donne à croire que la «stuga» date du 18e siècle, ce type de bâtiment dont le toit du corps central est couvert d'une toison herbeuse, remonte au Moyen Age. A l'intérieur, la Kyrkhultsstugan s'avère très spacieuse et, en observant de près son imposant foyer équipé d'un four à pain, son mobilier robuste et ses tapisseries et décorations murales aux motifs folkloriques, on comprend la «richesse» de ses anciens habitants. Dans la chambre à coucher, la symétrie parfaite d'une paire de lits d'alcôve garnis de rideaux à carreaux, évoque pour nous le romantisme d'une époque lointaine, à jamais disparue.

The grass growing on the roof protects the house from the wet and cold.

Das Gras, das auf dem Dach wächst, schützt das Bauwerk vor den Unbilden der Witterung und der eisigen Kälte.

L'herbe qui pousse sur le toit protège la construction contre les intempéries et le froid glacial.

ABOVE: *The walls of the main room are covered with rustic tapestries and decorations. The tables and chairs were made by a local craftsman, who was probably also responsible for the grandfather clock, or "moraklokka".*

RIGHT: *The fireplace was enormous and probably heated the entire house.*

FACING PAGE: *The housewife would sit under the skylight, darning and repairing her family's clothes or patiently spinning wool.*

OBEN: *Teppiche und andere Dekorationen mit volkstümlichen Motiven schmücken die Wände des Hauptraums. Die rustikalen Tische und Stühle stammen von einem ortsansässigen Kunsthandwerker, der wohl auch mit der großen »moraklokka«, der Standuhr, beauftragt worden war.*

RECHTS: *Die riesige Feuerstelle dient auch zur Beheizung.*

RECHTE SEITE: *Im Licht, das das Dachfenster spendete, flickte die Hausherrin und verbrachte Stunden damit, Wolle zu spinnen.*

CI-DESSUS: *Les murs de la pièce principale sont couverts de tapisseries et de décorations à thème folklorique. Les tables et les chaises rustiques sont l'œuvre d'un artisan local probablement aussi chargé d'exécuter la grande «moraklokka», l'horloge de grand-mère.*

A DROITE: *Le foyer est immense et sert aussi à chauffer la maison.*

PAGE DE DROITE: *C'est sous la lucarne que la maîtresse de maison réparait et reprisait les vêtements de sa famille et passait des heures à filer la laine.*

WALDEMARSUDDE
Prins Eugen
Stockholm

"Do you remember when I told you I was thinking of buying a place at Djurgården?" wrote Prince Eugene of Sweden in December 1899, to a friend. "Well, it's a wonderful spot, with shimmering sunsets and water and fine-looking boats. One of the houses would be perfect for my studio – it has a terrace in front, perfect for flowers. I'll grow flowers there." The youngest son of King Oscar II and Queen Sofia, Prince Eugene was attracted to an artistic career early in his life. After periods in Paris, Norway, Italy and Greece, he settled down at Waldemarsudde, a property surrounded by the bays of Ryssviken and Saltsjön, where he had a villa built by the architect Ferdinand Boberg. Until his death in 1947, this aesthete and scholar collected the works of his contemporaries – Zorn, Rodin, Bourdelle, Eldh, Milles, Larsson and Josephson – and painted on his own account in his gigantic studio, gathering around him the cream of Sweden's artistic and political world and tending his flowers. On his death, the man who said that next to art, flowers are what delight him most, bequeathed Waldemarsudde to the Swedish state, in the hope that posterity would share his passion – and it does.

In the dining room, an 18th-century obelisk-clock stands on the marble top of a gilded console table, dating from the same period.

Im Speisesaal steht eine obeliskenförmige Uhr aus dem 18. Jahrhundert auf der Marmorplatte einer vergoldeten Holzanrichte, die derselben Epoche entstammt.

Dans la salle à manger, une pendule 18ᵉ en forme d'obélisque est posée sur la tablette en marbre d'une console en bois doré de la même époque.

»Erinnern Sie sich, dass ich Ihnen erzählte, ich spielte mit dem Gedanken, eine Besitzung in Djurgården zu erwerben?«, schrieb Prinz Eugen von Schweden im Dezember 1899 an einen Freund. »Es ist ein wundersamer Ort, mit flirrenden Sonnenuntergängen, glitzerndem Wasser und eindrucksvollen Booten. Eines der Häuser wird perfekt sein, um darin mein Atelier unterzubringen – nach vorne hat es eine Terrasse, die zum Blumenzüchten ideal ist.« Prinz Eugen, Sohn von König Oskar II. und Königin Sofia, fühlte sich früh zur Künstlerlaufbahn hingezogen. Nach Aufenthalten in Paris, Norwegen, Italien und Griechenland ließ er sich in Waldermarsudde nieder, wo er durch den Architekten Ferdinand Boberg eine Villa errichten ließ. Bis zu seinem Tod 1947 sammelte dieser Ästhet und Gelehrte die Werke seiner Zeitgenossen Zorn, Rodin, Bourdelle, Eldh, Milles, Larsson und Josephson, während er selber in seinem riesigen Atelier malte, die feinsten Geister aus Kunst und Politik um sich scharte und sich mit Liebe um seine Blumen kümmerte. Prinz Eugen vermachte Waldemarsudde dem Staat, um Sorge zu tragen, dass seine Passion für die Schönheit der breiteren Öffentlichkeit zugänglich werde.

ABOVE: *The terrace was embellished in 1905 with a copy of the "Winged Victory of Samothrace".*
FOLLOWING PAGES: *The prince always gave pride of place to his own special treasures.*

OBEN: *1905 wurde die Terrasse mit einer Kopie der »Nike von Samothrake« verschönert.*
FOLGENDE DOPPELSEITE: *Der Prinz fand stets einen Ehrenplatz für seine Kostbarkeiten.*

CI-DESSUS: *Côté sud, la terrasse a été embellie en 1905 avec une copie de la «Victoire de Samothrace».*
DOUBLE PAGE SUIVANTE: *Le prince a toujours trouvé une place d'honneur pour ses trésors.*

«Vous vous souvenez que je vous racontais chérir l'idée d'acquérir une propriété à Djurgården?», écrit le prince Eugène de Suède en décembre 1899, à un ami. «C'est un endroit merveilleux, avec des couchers de soleil vibrants, une eau scintillante et des bateaux impressionnants. Une des maisons sera parfaite pour y loger mon atelier – elle a une terrasse devant, idéale pour cultiver des fleurs. J'y cultiverai mes fleurs …» Fils cadet du roi Oscar II et de la reine Sofia, le prince Eugène fut très tôt attiré par la carrière artistique. Après des séjours à Paris, en Norvège, en Italie et en Grèce, il s'établit à Waldemarsudde, un domaine cerné par les eaux de la baie de Ryssviken et du Saltsjön, et y fit construire une villa par l'architecte Ferdinand Boberg. Jusqu'à sa mort en 1947, cet esthète et érudit collectionna les œuvres de ses contemporains – Zorn, Rodin, Bourdelle, Eldh, Milles, Larsson et Josephson –, peignant lui-même dans son immense atelier, réunissant la fine fleur du monde artistique et politique et s'occupant de ses fleurs avec amour. L'homme qui avouait: «Après l'art, ce sont les fleurs qui m'enchantent le plus», a légué Waldemarsudde à l'Etat, soucieux de partager sa passion pour la beauté avec le grand public.

The Temple of Echo, built to a design by the prince himself, offers a fine view of the Saltsjön with the shores of Stockholm in the distance.

Der nach einem Entwurf des Prinzen erbaute Echo-Tempel bietet eine herrliche Aussicht auf den Saltsjön und auf die fernen Ufer von Stockholm.

Le Temple de l'Echo construit d'après un dessin du prince offre une vue splendide sur le Saltsjön et sur les rives lointaines de Stockholm.

PREVIOUS PAGES: *In the salons, paintings by Zorn and Larsson are combined with Gustavian and Empire furniture.*
ABOVE: *Each day, an army of gardeners makes sure that "the prince's flowers" continue to brighten his rooms.*
RIGHT: *a view of one of the greenhouses.*
FACING PAGE: *a small keeper's house, on the shores of the Saltsjön at the end of the garden.*

VORHERGEHENDE DOPPELSEITE: *In den Salons gesellen sich Gemälde von Zorn und Larsson zu Möbeln des gustavianischen und des Empire-Zeitalters.*
OBEN: *Täglich sorgt ein Heer von Gärtnern dafür, dass die Salons mit den »Blumen des Prinzen« geschmückt werden.*
RECHTS: *Blick in eines der Gewächshäuser.*
RECHTE SEITE: *Am Ende des Gartens trotzt ein Wärterhäuschen dem Gewässer des Saltsjön.*

DOUBLE PAGE PRÉCÉDENTE: *Dans les salons, des tableaux de Zorn et de Larsson côtoient un mobilier gustavien et Empire.*
CI-DESSUS: *Chaque jour, une armée de jardiniers veille à ce que les «fleurs du prince» embellissent les salons.*
A DROITE: *une vue sur une des serres.*
PAGE DE DROITE: *Au bout du jardin, une petite maison de gardien défie les eaux du Saltsjön.*

VARPET

Stockholm södra skärgård

It took courage to buy and restore this dilapidated turn-of-the-century house, which sits miraculously on one of the many islands of the Stockhom södra skärgård, a Baltic archipelago southeast of Stockholm. Nevertheless, for those who know the determined and enterprising family who now live there, the outcome was never in doubt; the resurrection of Varpet was bound to happen. Today, the handsome yellow and white building overlooks the island from the summit of its green hill; to reach it you have to moor your boat at the dock and trudge up a narrow, winding path. Once there, you discover that everything possible has been done to preserve the 1900's feel of the place. The lady of the house is pleased to say that she found all the original furniture in the cellar and restored it to its original freshness with a coat of white paint. The walls are vanilla-coloured and the chairs and sofas are upholstered in yellow-and-white checked fabric. The lamps all date from the Belle Epoque, and the décor is completed by white-tiled stoves and *pâte de verre* vases filled with nasturtiums – proving, if proof were needed, how well the elegance of the past blends with the present atmosphere of this lovely, quiet place.

PREVIOUS PAGES: *Each small island possessed its own jetty, with a cabin for fishing tackle, garden furniture and bathing costumes.*
LEFT: *the old rainwater butt.*

VORHERGEHENDE DOPPELSEITE: *Jedes Inselchen hat einen Anlegesteg und eine Hütte, in der das Angelgerät, die Gartenmöbel und das unentbehrliche Badezeug verstaut werden.*
LINKS: *Das Regenwasser wird in einem alten Fass aufgefangen.*

DOUBLE PAGE PRÉCÉDENTE: *Chaque îlot possède un embarcadère et une cabane où on range le matériel de pêche, les meubles de jardin et l'indispensable maillot de bain.*
A GAUCHE: *L'eau de pluie est recueillie dans un vieux tonneau.*

An island home, a place of enchantment.

Wer würde nicht gerne in diesem Haus und auf dieser Zauberinsel leben?

Qui ne voudrait pas vivre dans cette maison et sur cette île enchantée?

Es war mutig, sehr mutig, es zu erwerben und zu restaurieren, jenes zerfallene Jahrhundertwendehaus, das wie durch ein Wunder auf einer der zahlreichen Inseln des Stockholm södra skärgård, einem Archipel im Südosten Stockholms, steht. Wer allerdings diese entschlossene und unternehmungslustige Familie kennt, für den gab es keinen Zweifel: die Wiederbelebung von Varpet war nur eine Frage der Zeit. Heute überragt das schöne gelbweiße Bauwerk von der Höhe seines grünen Hügels herab die Insel und mit dem Boot am weißen Steg anzulegen, ehe man den schmalen Schlängelpfad zum Haus »bewältigt«, bleibt ein unvergessliches Erlebnis. Die Hausherrin hat alles getan, um den Charakter des Anwesens zu wahren. Stolz verweist sie darauf, dass sie die Originalmöbel im Keller gefunden und ihnen ihre blütenweiße Farbe zurückgegeben hat. Wände in Vanilleton, mit gelbweißem Karostoff bezogene Stühle und Kanapees, Lampen der Belle Époque, weiße Kachelöfen und Vasen mit Kresse runden das geschmackvolle Dekor ab und belegen, so überhaupt nötig, dass die Vergangenheit mit der heiteren Insel in bestem Einklang steht.

On the porch at Varpet – a bowl of fruit and a bouquet of flowers in a vase.

Die Obstschale und der Blumenstrauß unter dem Portalvorbau lassen erkennen, dass man es sich in Varpet gut gehen lässt!

Sous le porche, une coupe de fruits et un bouquet dans un vase trahissent qu'il fait bon vivre à Varpet!

Il leur fallut du courage, beaucoup de courage, des tonnes de courage pour acquérir et se mettre à restaurer cette vétuste maison «fin de siècle» posée comme par miracle sur une des nombreuses îles du Stockholm södra skärgård, l'archipel situé au sud-est de Stockholm. Néanmoins, pour ceux qui connaissent bien cette famille déterminée et entreprenante, la chose ne faisait aucun doute: la résurrection de Varpet n'était qu'une question de temps. Aujourd'hui, la belle construction jaune et blanche domine l'île du haut de sa colline verdoyante et amarrer son bateau à l'embarcadère blanc avant de «grimper» l'étroit chemin sinueux qui mène vers la maison reste une expérience inoubliable. La maîtresse des lieux a tout mis en œuvre pour préserver le côté 1900 de sa demeure. Elle se vante d'avoir trouvé le mobilier original dans la cave et de lui avoir rendu sa blancheur pimpante et fraîche. Des murs couleur vanille, des chaises et des canapés recouverts d'un tissu à carreaux blancs et jaunes, des lampes Belle Epoque, des poêles en faïence blanche et des vases en pâte de verre remplis de nasturtiums complètent ce décor délicat et prouvent, s'il en était besoin, qu'un retour au passé s'accommode à merveille d'une île sereine où règne la beauté.

ABOVE AND FACING
PAGE: *In the sitting
room, the white-lac-
quered furniture, the
yellow walls, the built-
in cupboards and the
benches reflect the taste
of the first decade of the
20th century.*
RIGHT: *the kitchen,
snug and old-fashioned.*
FOLLOWING PAGES:
*Fruit season: the pots
of jam are still warm
from the sterilizer, and
in extremis a branch
broken from the apple
tree finds a berth in a
wash-jug.*

OBEN UND RECHTE
SEITE: *Das weiß-
lackierte Mobiliar, die
gelben Wände, die Sitz-
bank und die einge-
lassenen Schränke im
Wohnzimmer spiegeln
den Geschmack der
1910er Jahre wider.*
RECHTS: *Man möchte
meinen, man sei in
Omas Küche!*
FOLGENDE DOPPEL-
SEITE: *Es ist Obst-
saison, wie die noch
warmen Marmeladen-
gläser und der Apfel-
zweig im Krug zeigen.*

CI-DESSUS ET PAGE
DE DROITE: *Dans le
séjour, le mobilier laqué
blanc, les murs jaunes,
la banquette et les
armoires encastrées
reflètent le goût des
années 1910.*
A DROITE: *On se croi-
rait dans la cuisine de
grand-mère!*
DOUBLE PAGE SUI-
VANTE: *La saison des
fruits bat son plein, en
témoignent les pots de
confiture encore tièdes et
la branche de pommier
dans un broc.*

LEFT: *An old wash-basin, an earthenware jug, a venerable looking glass – what more do you need for basic ablutions?*

LINKS: *Ein alter Waschtisch, ein Steingutkrug und ein alter Spiegel: Was braucht es mehr für die Körperpflege?*

A GAUCHE: *Un vieux lavabo, une cruche en faïence et un miroir ancien: que faut-il de plus pour faire sa toilette?*

FACING PAGE: *A ray of sunshine lingers on the twin bedsteads and the embroidered counterpane trimmed with lace.*
RIGHT: *The attic bathroom overlooks the terrace – the colours here were chosen by the mistress of the house.*

LINKE SEITE: *Über das Doppelbett aus lackiertem Metall mit seiner bestickten und spitzenbesetzten Decke streift ein Sonnenstrahl.*
RECHTS: *Das Badezimmer im Dachgeschoss geht auf eine Terrasse hinaus. Die Farben hat die Hausherrin ausgesucht.*

PAGE DE GAUCHE: *Un rayon de soleil s'attarde sur les lits jumeaux en métal laqué et sur la couverture ancienne, brodée et garnie de dentelles.*
A DROITE: *La salle de bains sous les combles donne sur une grande terrasse. La maîtresse de maison en a choisi les couleurs.*

$\mathcal{W}$RETA GESTGIFVERI

Södermanland

How to translate the word "gestgifveri"? Is it a tavern, a posting inn, or a place that merely offers hospitality? Jim Grundström and his partners prefer the latter definition, and in converting their pretty abandoned "gestvifveri" they have realised an old dream of receiving guests in an ambience of perfect calm and beauty. The origins of the place go back to the 14th-century, and the house was already an establishment of some repute as long ago as 1666. In its time it sheltered and fed such figures as Linnaeus, Count Axel von Fersen (the "Beau Fersen" who fell in love with Queen Marie-Antoinette) and the future King of Sweden, Jean-Baptiste Bernadotte. Sadly, by 1995 nothing remained of its former glory; the place had come to an inglorious pass as a turkey farm and motorbike repair shop. But Jim Grundström has talent and taste in abundance, and under his sure direction the "gestgifveri" was gradually transformed into an elegant manor filled with Gustavian furniture, family portraits, comfortable beds and sofas, a dream dining room and thoroughly 21st-century comforts cunningly concealed. Thanks to its saviour, Wreta gestgifveri has recovered all of its former beauty – and more.

A Gustavian gilded looking-glass with a candle-sconce – a recent copy of an antique original – hangs on the bedroom wall.

Im Schlafzimmer hängt ein vergoldeter Spiegel im gustavianischen Stil mit Kerzenhalter, eine Nachbildung aus heutiger Zeit.

Un miroir gustavien doré, équipé d'un bras de lumière – une réédition récente – est accroché dans la chambre à coucher.

Wie soll man das Wort »gestgifveri« übersetzen? Ist es eine »Herberge«, ein »Rasthaus« oder ein »Ort, wo man Gastfreundschaft pflegt«? Jim Grundström und seine Partner bevorzugen die letztgenannte Version, denn als sie diese hübsche verlassene »gestgifveri« restaurierten, erfüllten sie sich einen alten Traum: Gäste in einer Atmosphäre vollkommener Ruhe und Schönheit zu empfangen. Die Anfänge der Herberge reichen bis ins 14. Jahrhundert zurück, und 1666 stieg Wreta zum renommierten »Rasthaus« auf. Den Ruf als Luxusherberge erwarb es sich freilich, als dort Persönlichkeiten wie Carl von Linné, Graf Axel von Fersen und der spätere schwedische König Jean-Baptiste Bernadotte logierten und tafelten. Von diesem alten Ruhm war 1995 nichts mehr zu spüren. Wreta war zur Truthahnzucht und Mopedwerkstatt heruntergewirtschaftet worden. Da jedoch bei Grundström guter Geschmack und Talent zusammenkommen, hat die »gestgifveri« sich nach und nach zu einem eleganten Herrenhaus gemausert, dessen Räumlichkeiten Mobiliar im gustavianischen Stil, Familienportraits, bequeme Betten und Kanapees sowie einen traumhaften Speisesaal beherbergen und mit kunstvoll verborgenem hochmodernem Komfort aufwarten.

Comment traduire le mot «Gestgifveri»? Est-ce une «auberge», un «relais» ou un «endroit où on vous offre l'hospitalité»? Jim Grundström et ses partenaires préféreront la dernière solution, car en restaurant cette jolie «gestgifveri» abandonnée, ils ont réalisé un très vieux rêve: recevoir des hôtes dans une ambiance de calme et de beauté parfaite. Les origines de l'auberge remontent au 14e siècle et Wreta devint un «relais» renommé en 1666. Mais c'est en offrant le gîte et le couvert à des personnalités comme le naturaliste Carl von Linné, le comte Axel von Fersen (le «Beau Fersen» qui s'éprit de Marie-Antoinette) et le futur roi de Suède Jean-Baptiste Bernadotte, que le relais acquit sa réputation d'auberge de luxe. En 1995, plus rien ne subsistait de cette ancienne gloire – Wreta avait terminé sa carrière comme élevage de dindons et atelier de réparation de cyclomoteurs –, mais comme Grundström joint le bon goût au talent, la «gestgifveri» s'est transformée petit à petit en un manoir élégant dont les salons accueillent un mobilier gustavien, des portraits de famille, des lits et des canapés douillets, une salle à manger de rêve et un confort très 21e siècle habilement dissimulé. Grâce à son sauveteur, la Wreta gestgifveri a retrouvé son allure d'antan.

LEFT: *In the entrance an early 19th-century portrait of a lady rests on a rustic chest of drawers. The dining room beyond has been decorated in 18th-century style.*

FACING PAGE: *A few steps from the "skriv-kammare" (office), a table and chair from the 18th century offer an ideal spot to read, write or simply sit and let the magic of the place envelop you.*

LINKS: *Auf der rusti-kalen Kommode in der Diele steht ein Portrait einer Dame aus der Zeit des Biedermeier. Die Tür öffnet sich zum Esszimmer, das im Stil des 18. Jahrhunderts eingerichtet ist.*

RECHTE SEITE: *Ein paar Schritte von der »skrivkammare« – dem Büro – entfernt stößt man auf einen Tisch und einen Stuhl aus dem 18. Jahrhundert, die zum Lesen oder Schreiben einladen, oder auch dazu, sich einfach der Faszination des Ortes zu überlassen.*

A GAUCHE: *Dans l'entrée une commode campagnarde sert de support à un portrait de femme d'époque Bieder-meier. La porte s'ouvre sur une salle à manger décorée dans le plus pur goût 18ᵉ.*

PAGE DE DROITE: *Près de la «skrivkam-mare» – le bureau – on découvre une table et une chaise 18ᵉ qui invi-tent les hôtes à lire, à écrire ou, simplement, à s'imprégner de l'am-biance magique des lieux.*

In the dining room,
time seems to stand still:
the year is 1750, and the
chairs await a group of
guests in long-skirted
riding coats, powdered
wigs and three-cornered
hats.

Im Speisesaal ist die
Zeit stehen geblieben:
Der Kalender zeigt das
Jahr 1750 an und es ist,
als erwarte man Gäste
im Gehrock, den Drei-
spitz locker auf die
gepuderte Perücke
gestülpt …

Dans la salle à manger,
le temps s'est arrêté : le
calendrier marque l'an-
née 1750 et on semble
attendre des invités en
redingote, le tricorne
légèrement posé sur la
perruque poudrée …

ABOVE: *In the large grey and white "matsal", the tablecloths are all made of pure white linen. The long central table is set with white and gold china, pewter candlesticks and antique terrines.*
RIGHT: *the bedroom, decorated throughout in 18th-century country style.*
FACING PAGE: *a simple but immaculate table setting.*

OBEN: *Die Tische im geräumigen, weißgrau Ton-in-Ton gehaltenen »matsal« sind mit weißem Leinen gedeckt. Weißgoldenes Porzellan, Zinnleuchter und alte Terrinen harren auf dem langen Tisch in der Mitte der Gäste.*
RECHTS: *das ganz im ländlichen Stil des 18. Jahrhunderts dekorierte Schlafzimmer.*
RECHTE SEITE: *ein schmucker Tisch für die Freuden des Gaumens und zum Augenschmaus.*

CI-DESSUS: *Dans la vaste «matsal» décorée d'un camaïeu de gris et de blancs, les tables sont nappées de lin blanc. Sur la longue table centrale, la porcelaine blanc et or, les bougeoirs en étain et les terrines anciennes attendent les invités.*
A DROITE: *la chambre à coucher, décorée entièrement dans un style campagnard du 18e siècle.*
PAGE DE DROITE: *une belle tablée, pour le plaisir des papilles et celui des yeux.*

$\mathcal{L}$ÖFSTAD SLOTT

Östergötland

One night in January 1750, a serving girl lodged in one of the out-buildings of the manor at Löfstad forgot to put out her candle. The ensuing conflagration spread rapidly to the big house, reducing the residence of the De La Gardie family to smoking ashes. The new owner, Count von Fersen, built a new "slott" in the neo-classical style without embellishments. In this house, the main innovation for the period consisted in the installation of the kitchen and the servants' quarters in the basement of the building, a thoroughly modern thing to do. In 1926, Countess Emilie, the last descendant of the Piper family, died and bequeathed the house and its contents to the Östergötland County Museum and the Swedish House of Nobility – stipulating that her home should not be changed in any respect and that its interior, furnishings and objects must be kept intact. Today, Löfstad seems to await the imminent return of "fröken" Emilie: her afternoon tea is waiting for her in her bed-room, her hat and overcoat lie ready for her daily constitutional, and apparently the kitchen, dining room and maids' rooms are all a-bustle.

In einer Januarnacht des Jahres 1750 vergaß eine Dienerin in einem der Nebengebäude des Landschlosses von Löfstad, ihre Kerze zu löschen. Das Feuer breitete sich rasch bis zum Hauptgebäude aus und verwandelte den Sitz der De La Gardie in rauchende Asche. Der neue Besitzer, der Graf von Fersen, ließ das neue »slott« in einem schnörkellosen klassizistischem Stil erbauen. Die eigentliche Neuheit für die damalige Zeit bestand darin, dass er Küchen und Gesindeunterkünfte im Untergeschoss des Gebäudes einrichten ließ, was von einer sehr »modernen« Auffassung zeugt. Als die letzte Nachfahrin der Piper, die Gräfin Emilie, 1926 verstarb, vermachte sie das Schloss und seinen Inhalt dem Museum von Östergötland und dem »House of Nobility«, unter der Auflage, dass die Baulichkeiten keine Veränderung erführen und die Interieurs, das Mobiliar und die Einrichtungsgegenstände unangetastet blieben. Heute scheint Löfstad die baldige Wiederkehr von »fröken« Emilie zu erwarten: Man hat ihr das Tablett mit dem »afternoon-tea« aufs Zimmer gestellt; ihr Hut und ihr Ausgehrock liegen für den Spaziergang bereit und in Küche, Speisesaal und Gesindekammern herrscht rege Betriebsamkeit.

En une nuit de janvier de l'année 1750, une servante logée dans une des dépendances du manoir de Löfstad, oublia d'éteindre sa chandelle et l'incendie se propagea très rapidement jusqu'au manoir, réduisant la résidence des De La Gardie en un tas de cendres fumantes. Le nouveau propriétaire, le comte von Fersen, fit construire le nouveau «slott» dans un style néoclassique sans fioritures. En fait, la véritable innovation pour l'époque fut d'installer les cuisines et des logements pour les domestiques dans les sous-sols du bâtiment, ce qui, aujourd'hui, témoigne d'un esprit très «moderne». En 1926, la comtesse Emilie, dernière descendante des Piper, mourut et légua le manoir et son contenu au Musée Municipal du Östergötland et à l'Association des Nobles, stipulant que la demeure ne subirait aucun changement et qu'on ne toucherait point aux intérieurs, au mobilier et aux objets. Aujourd'hui, Löfstad semble attendre le retour imminent de «fröken» Emilie: on a fait monter le plateau avec son «afternoon-tea» dans sa chambre; son chapeau et sa redingote sont préparés pour l'heure de la promenade et la cuisine, la salle à manger et les chambres de bonnes grouillent à nouveau d'une activité fiévreuse.

ABOVE: *Tea-time in the music room, with rows of ancestors solemnly looking on.*
RIGHT: *There are still lifes everywhere you look in this house – a pretty painting, a fine piece of old furniture, assorted unpretentious bibelots.*
FACING PAGE: *a silver tray, set for the Countess's frugal breakfast.*

OBEN: *Im Musiksalon hat die Stunde für den Tee geschlagen. Die Ahnen in ihren vergoldeten Rahmen werden die stummen Zeugen abgeben …*
RECHTS: *Allenthalben stößt der begeisterte Besucher auf spontane Still-Leben – ein hübsches Gemälde, ein altes Möbelstück, ein paar unprätentiöse Nippessachen …*
RECHTE SEITE: *Auf dem Silbertablett harrt ein frugales Frühstück der Gräfin.*

CI-DESSUS: *Dans le salon de musique, l'heure du thé a sonné. Les ancêtres dans leurs cadres lourdement dorés en seront les témoins taciturnes …*
A DROITE: *Partout le visiteur enchanté découvre des natures mortes spontanées – un joli tableau, un meuble ancien, quelques bibelots sans prétention …*
PAGE DE DROITE: *Le plateau en argent chargé d'un petit déjeuner frugal attend la comtesse.*

LEFT: *A broad passage-way in the basement serves as the laundry, with wardrobes and cupboards for storing various utensils.*
FACING PAGE: *The castle had only one bathroom, for the exclu-sive use of the Countess; when she went down there on Friday evenings the servants were expect-ed to stay well out of sight.*

LINKS: *Im Souterrain dient ein breiter Korri-dor mit Schränken und Spinden, in denen diverse Gerätschaften verstaut waren, als Waschküche.*
RECHTE SEITE: *Das Schloss hatte nur ein Badezimmer, nämlich das der Gräfin. Wenn sie es am Freitagabend aufsuchte, hatten die Domestiken sich nicht blicken zu lassen …*

A GAUCHE: *Un large corridor fait office de buanderie au sous-sol et abrite les armoires et les placards où on rangeait des ustensiles divers.*
PAGE DE DROITE: *Le château n'avait qu'une seule salle de bains – celle de la comtesse – et lorsqu'elle y descendait le vendredi soir, les domestiques étaient censés se rendre invi-sibles …*

Hörle Herrgård

Småland

That Ingrid Böhn Jullander has a right to be proud of her beautiful property becomes quite clear when you see the manor at Hörle she fought so hard to save. Built in 1746 by the architect Bengt Wilhelm Carlberg, titular architect of the city of Göteborg, Hörle herrgård was originally lived in by Anna Margareta Lilliecreutz, who occupied its elegant salons with her third husband Gabriel von Seth. The Böhn family temporarily reconstructed the décor at Hörle herrgård in 1992, using very fine Gustavian furniture in homage to the architect Carl Hårleman, the original creator of the interiors. The Böhns chose 1771 as their point of departure, since it was in that year that the house's first occupant died. To recreate the original rich but restrained décor, they have tapped freely into a private collection and Hörle herrgård became a veritable window onto the past, with rococo sofas covered with checked fabrics, a four-poster bed and armchairs upholstered in Indian blue and white materials, plaster busts and a modest kitchen equipped with china from the Compagnie des Indes. Truly a completely new lease of life for a 250-year-old "grand old lady" of a house.

A bowl with a blue and white lid marries perfectly with the rustic Gustavian table and the floral fabric – the original of the latter was in the manor of Ekebyholm during the 18th century.

Die Schüssel mit weiß-blauem Deckel passt perfekt zu dem rustikalen Tisch im gustavianischen Stil und dem mit floralen Ornamenten durchwirkten Stoff, dessen Original im 18. Jahrhundert Gut Ekebyholm verschönerte.

Le pot à couvercle bleu et blanc se marie parfaitement avec la table rustique gustavienne et avec le tissu floral dont l'original embellissait, au 18ᵉ siècle, le manoir d'Ekebyholm.

The façade of Hörle
herrgård, built in 1746
by the architect Bengt
Wilhelm Carlberg.

Die Fassade von Hörle
herrgård, erbaut 1746
von dem Architekten
Bengt Wilhelm Carl-
berg.

La façade de Hörle
herrgård, construit en
1746 par l'architecte
Bengt Wilhelm Carl-
berg.

The façade of Hörle
herrgård, built in 1746
by the architect Bengt
Wilhelm Carlberg.

Die Fassade von Hörle
herrgård, erbaut 1746
von dem Architekten
Bengt Wilhelm Carl-
berg.

La façade de Hörle
herrgård, construit en
1746 par l'architecte
Bengt Wilhelm Carl-
berg.

Ingrid Böhn Jullander ist zu Recht stolz auf ihr schönes Anwesen in Hörle und wenn man ihr Herrengut sieht, leuchtet ein, warum sie sich mit Leib und Seele für dessen Erhaltung eingesetzt hat. 1746 durch den Göteborger Stadtarchitekten Bengt Wilhelm Carlberg erbaut, wurde Hörle herrgård von Anna Margareta Lilliecreutz bewohnt, die mit ihrem (dritten) Gemahl Gabriel von Seth die eleganten Salons des Hauses belebte. Die Familie Böhn rekonstruierte die Innendekoration ihres Besitzes 1992. Dabei konnte sie zeitweilig auf gustavianisches Mobiliar von bemerkenswerter Qualität zurückgreifen – eine Hommage an den Architekten Carl Hårleman, der die Inneneinrichtung des »herrgård« schuf. Zum Ausgangspunkt nahmen die Böhns das Jahr 1771, in dem die erste Bewohnerin verstorben war. Zur Wiederherstellung der luxuriösen, aber sehr schlichten Dekoration schöpften sie ausgiebig aus einer Privatsammlung. So ist Hörle herrgård zu einem Fenster in die Vergangenheit geworden, bereichert um Rokoko-Kanapees mit Karobezügen, ein Himmelbett nebst Sesseln in blauem und weißem Baumwollsatin, dazu Gipsbüsten wie auch eine bescheidene Küche, die mit feinem Porzellan der Ostindischen Kompanie aufwartet.

Ingrid Böhn Jullander a raison d'être fière de sa belle propriété de Hörle et on comprend aisément en voyant son manoir pourquoi elle s'est battue corps et âme pour le préserver. Construit en 1746 par l'architecte Bengt Wilhelm Carlberg, architecte en titre de la ville de Göteborg, Hörle herrgård fut habité par Anna Margareta Lilliecreutz qui occupa ces salons élégants avec son (troisième) époux Gabrïel von Seth. La famille Böhn se félicite d'avoir reconstruit la décoration intérieure de sa propriété en 1992, en y introduisant temporairement un mobilier gustavien d'une qualité remarquable – un hommage à l'architecte Carl Hårleman qui créa les intérieurs du «herrgård». Les Böhn ont choisi comme point de départ l'année 1771, qui vit le décès de la première occupante. Pour recréer la décoration luxueuse mais très dépouillée, ils ont puisé librement dans une collection privée. Devenu une véritable fenêtre sur le passé, Hörle herrgård s'enrichit de canapés rococo garnis de tissus à carreaux, d'un lit à baldaquin et de fauteuils habillés d'indienne bleue et blanche, de bustes en plâtre et d'une cuisine modeste équipée d'une fine porcelaine de la Compagnie des Indes. Un vrai bain de jouvence pour une «vieille dame» âgée de deux siècles et demi.

The "china kitchen" has been reconstituted: this was a room where porcelain and blue and white earthenware used to be stored.

Die »Porzellanküche« konnte rekonstruiert werden. Hier waren einst das Porzellan und blauweiße Fayencen untergebracht.

La «cuisine aux porcelaines» a été reconstituée. C'est la pièce où l'on rangeait jadis les porcelaines et les faïences bleues et blanches.

LEFT: *In the dining room, the table, the rustic chairs and the bust are all copies, but the rococo chair and the chandelier date from the 18th century.*
FACING PAGE: *Near an alcove, books, a candlestick and a glass of "brännvin" for a moment of quiet.*

LINKS: *Tisch, rustikale Stühle und die Büste in diesem geräumigen Speisesaal sind Kopien, aber der Rokoko-Stuhl und der Lüster stammen aus dem 18. Jahrhundert.*
RECHTE SEITE: *In der Nähe des Alkovens laden Bücher, ein Kandelaber und ein Glas »brännvin« zur Entspannung ein.*

A GAUCHE: *Dans cette vaste salle à manger, la table, les sièges rustiques et le buste sont des copies, mais la chaise rococo et le lustre datent du 18e siècle.*
PAGE DE DROITE: *Près de l'alcôve, des livres, un chandelier et un verre de «brännvin» invitent à la détente.*

LEFT: *In one of the bedrooms, an 18th-century chair, sofa, and four-poster bed. The latter has been stripped of its curtains and counterpane.*
FACING PAGE: *a silk embroidered quilt, on a bed with a sumptuous damask canopy.*

LINKS: *In einem der Schlafzimmer sticht ein Himmelbett aus dem 18. Jahrhundert, von dem Vorgänge und Überwurf abgenommen wurden, aus einem Möbelensemble aus derselben Epoche hervor.*
RECHTE SEITE: *ein Bettüberwurf aus gepolsterter und bestickter Seide auf einem Prunkbett, über dem ein prachtvoller Himmel aus Seidendamast schwebt.*

A GAUCHE: *Dans une autre chambre, un lit à baldaquin 18ᵉ dépouillé de ses courtines et de son couvre-lit domine un ensemble de meubles de la même époque.*
PAGE DE DROITE: *un couvre-lit en soie matelassée et brodée sur un lit d'apparat garni d'un sompteux ciel de soie damassée.*

RIGHT: *This bed in its shallow alcove can be dismantled.*
FOLLOWING PAGES, LEFT: *In the pantry, simplicity is the key: nothing disturbs the absolute austerity of the décor.*
FOLLOWING PAGES, RIGHT: *The walls of Anna Margareta Lilliecreutz's bedroom are hung with an Indian print fabric like the ones at Ekebyholm.*

RECHTS: *Das Himmelbett in dem wenig tiefen Alkoven lässt sich auseinander nehmen.*
FOLGENDE DOPPELSEITE, LINKS: *Im Arbeitsraum herrscht Einfachheit, so dass nichts die Strenge des Dekors stört.*
FOLGENDE DOPPELSEITE, RECHTS: *Die Wände im Zimmer von Anna Margareta Lilliecreutz sind mit einem bedruckten Baumwollstoff bespannt, der den Wandschmuck von Gut Ekebyholm nachahmt.*

A DROITE: *Le lit à baldaquin dans l'alcôve peu profonde est démontable.*
DOUBLE PAGE SUIVANTE, À GAUCHE: *La simplicité règne dans l'office et rien ne vient troubler l'austérité du décor.*
DOUBLE PAGE SUIVANTE, À DROITE: *Les murs de la chambre d'Anna Margareta Lilliecreutz sont tendus d'une «indienne» imitant celles du manoir d'Ekebyholm.*

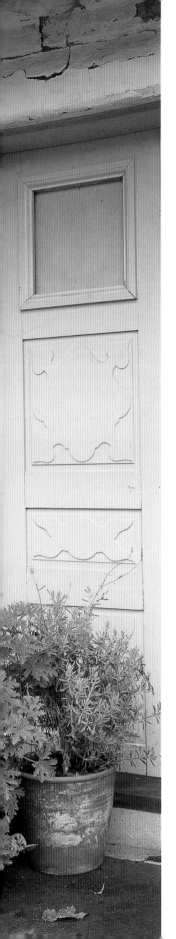

D ITTE CLASE OCH HANS MALMBORG

Skåne

The antique dealer Hans Malmborg and his wife Ditte smile when people ask them if they feel uncomfortable living so close to a cemetery. They know very well that discovering their isolated 200-year-old farmhouse was something of a miracle in itself. Even so, after friends had stumbled on the place by chance and told them about it, they waited for eight months before going over to visit. As soon as they did, they fell completely in love, not only with the little building but also with its odd surroundings. The house was hidden behind a row of 100-year-old trees, and the only adjoining features were a small white parish church and a graveyard. Today, the Malmborgs' home has everything needful for a couple of incorrigible romantics: small windows decorated with cotton curtains, geraniums, old wooden floorboards which creak beneath your feet, a small, intimate kitchen with bright red walls and low-ceilinged rooms filled with Gustavian furniture, English earthenware, and generalised pastel tones. In addition there is Isak, the fortunate baby of the house, who is six months old and destined to grow up in the authentic atmosphere created by his parents.

LEFT: *potted aromatic plants beside the front door.*
ABOVE: *the drive leading up to the house.*

LINKS: *In der Nähe der Eingangstür hat Ditte Töpfe mit duftenden Kräutern aufgestellt.*
OBEN: *die Allee, die zum Haus führt.*

A GAUCHE: *Ditte a placé des plantes aromatiques en pots près de la porte d'entrée.*
CI-DESSUS: *l'allée qui mène à la maison.*

Der Antiquitätenhändler Hans Malmborg und seine Frau Ditte lächeln leise, wenn man sie fragt, ob sie keine Angst hätten, neben einem Friedhof zu leben. Denn sie sind sich bewusst, dass es an ein Wunder grenzt, diesen zwei Jahrhunderte alten Bauernhof an einem entlegenen und sonderbaren Ort aufgestöbert zu haben. Dabei brauchten Ditte und Hans fast acht Monate, bis sie sich für das baufällige Gemäuer interessierten, auf das Freunde von ihnen zufällig gestoßen waren. Doch bei der ersten Besichtigung verliebten sie sich auf Anhieb rettungslos in das kleine Haus und seine ungewöhnliche Umgebung. Verborgen hinter einer Reihe Jahrhunderte alter Bäume, in der Nachbarschaft nichts als eine kleine weiße Kirche und einen »Acker der letzten Ruhe«, hat das Haus der Malmborgs alles, was unbeirrbar romantischen Gemütern gefallen muss: mit leichten Baumwollgardinen geschmückte Fenster, Geranien, einen alten Dielenboden, der unter den Füßen knarrt, eine anheimelnde Küche mit leuchtend roten Wänden, niedrige Räume, die durch Möbel im gustavianischen Stil, englische Fayencen und pastellene Farbtöne verschönt wurden. Und dann ist da noch Isak, der sechs Monate alte Nachwuchs. Ist es nicht wunderbar, in dieser Atmosphäre aufzuwachsen?

L'antiquaire Hans Malmborg et sa femme Ditte sourient finement quand on leur demande s'ils n'ont pas peur de vivre à l'ombre d'un cimetière. Ils sont en effet parfaitement conscients que le fait d'avoir déniché cette ferme bicentenaire dans un endroit isolé et indéniablement insolite tient du miracle. Ditte et Hans ont pourtant mis près de huit mois avant de s'intéresser à la bâtisse vétuste que des amis avaient découverte, par le plus grand des hasards. Mais lors de la première confrontation, ils sont tombés éperdument amoureux de la petite maison et de son environnement inhabituel. Cachée derrière une rangée d'arbres séculaires, n'ayant pour voisins qu'une petite église blanche et «un champ de l'éternel repos», la demeure des Malmborg a tout pour plaire aux âmes incorrigiblement romantiques: petites fenêtres garnies de rideaux en voile de coton, géraniums, un vieux plancher qui craque sous les pas, une petite cuisine intime aux murs rouge vif et des pièces basses embellies par des meubles gustaviens, des faïences anglaises et des tons pastels. Et puis il y a Isak, le bébé de la maison, âgé de six mois. N'est-ce pas merveilleux de pouvoir grandir dans cette ambiance authentique créée de main de maître par ses parents?

LEFT: *The tiles on the floor of the "new" kitchen come from a neighbouring farmhouse. Hans built the sink and shelves himself.*
FACING PAGE: *Ditte insisted on painting the kitchen walls with a dark wine-coloured wash. This goes well with the Delft tiles, the blue and white earthenware and the pretty enamelled coffee pot.*

LINKS: *Die Fliesen in der »neuen« Küche stammen aus einem alten Bauernhof in der Umgebung. Spüle und Unterschränke hat Hans selbst gebaut.*
RECHTE SEITE: *Ditte bestand darauf, dass die Wände ihrer Küche weinrot getüncht würden. Diese Farbe passt perfekt zu den Delfter Kacheln, den blauweißen Fayencen und der hübschen emaillierten Kaffeekanne.*

A GAUCHE: *Le carrelage de la «nouvelle» cuisine provient d'une ancienne ferme des environs. Hans a construit l'évier et les rangements.*
PAGE DE DROITE: *Ditte a insisté pour que les murs de sa cuisine soient couverts d'un lavis lie-de-vin. Cette couleur se marie parfaitement avec les carrelages en Delft, les faïences bleues et blanches et la jolie cafetière émaillée.*

FACING PAGE: *The rustic table and chairs date from the 19th century.*

ABOVE: *In the old days, the sitting room was only used for family gatherings, which took place on Sundays. The Malmborgs have turned this beautiful, light-filled space with its comfortable English sofa into the warm heart of their house.*

RIGHT: *The walls of the bedroom are covered in a blue wash, which gives added emphasis to the 19th-century chair, the Gustavian gilt clock and the bed with its white linen hangings.*

LINKE SEITE: *Der rustikale Tisch und die Stühle stammen aus dem 19. Jahrhundert.*

OBEN: *Früher war das Wohnzimmer den sonntäglichen Familienzusammenkünften vorbehalten. Doch für die Malmborgs bildet dieser helle Raum mit dem bequemen englischen Sofa das wahre Herzstück des Hauses.*

RECHTS: *Ein blauer Anstrich bedeckt die Wände des Schlafzimmers, von dem sich ein Stuhl aus dem 19. Jahrhundert und eine vergoldete gustavianische Pendeluhr vorteilhaft abheben.*

PAGE DE GAUCHE: *La table et les chaises rustiques datent du 19ᵉ siècle.*

CI-DESSUS: *Jadis, le séjour était réservé aux réunions de famille du dimanche, mais pour les Malmborg cette belle pièce claire au confortable canapé anglais est le véritable cœur de la maison.*

A DROITE: *Un lavis bleu couvre les murs de la chambre à coucher et met en valeur une chaise 19ᵉ, une pendule dorée gustavienne et un lit drapé de lin blanc.*

LEFT: *Hans built the bathroom in the barn. The rustic nature of the room is accentuated by the way the basin is set into bricks, which have been covered in plaster and painted yellow ochre.*

LINKS: *Hans hat das Badezimmer in der Scheune eingerichtet. Der rustikale Charakter des Raums wird betont durch die Waschbeckeneinfassung aus Backstein, die verputzt und ockergelb getüncht wurde.*

A GAUCHE: *Hans a installé la salle de bains dans la grange. Le caractère rustique de la pièce est accentué par l'encastrement de lavabo en briques recouvert de stuc et badigeonné d'ocre jaune.*

FACING PAGE: *on the bathroom windowsill, a plant with its leaves canted toward the sunlight.*
RIGHT: *The cast-iron enamelled bathtub dates from the early 20th century. The pipes are masked by the base of a Medici vase.*

LINKE SEITE: *Auf dem Fenstersims des Badezimmers wendet eine Pflanze ihre Blätter dem Licht zu.*
RECHTS: *Die gusseiserne Emaille-Badewanne stammt vom Anfang des 20. Jahrhunderts. Ein Sockel, auf dem eine Medici-Vase thront, verbirgt die Zuleitungen.*

PAGE DE GAUCHE: *Sur l'appui de fenêtre de la salle de bains, une plante tourne ses feuilles vers la lumière.*
A DROITE: *La baignoire en fonte émaillée date du début du 20ᵉ siècle. Un socle couronné d'un vase Médicis dissimule la tuyauterie.*

$\mathcal{A}$STRID LINDGREN

Småland

Few writers have captured the magic of childhood as Astrid Lindgren has done. Born in 1907 at Näs, a suburb of Vimmerby in the province of Småland, Astrid grew up on her parents' farm – a modest building painted the traditional bull's-blood hue. It was here, in the kitchen with its red and white checked curtains and oil lamp, that a small miracle took place: Little Astrid became enchanted with the fairy stories told to her by Edit, the daughter of a farm labourer, and through them discovered poetry and literature. Later, in Stockholm, Astrid herself began making up fairy stories for her daughter Karin, and by setting down on paper the adventures of such characters as Pippi Longstocking, Emil, Mardie, Karlsson and Ronia, the farmer's daughter was able to recreate the lost paradise of her childhood. It was a paradise that curiously resembled her father's house at Näs, where the children played until they were exhausted and where the parents contributed to the flowering of their children's personalities. Since 1998, Astrid's admirers have been able to visit the imaginary world she described at "Astrid Lindgrens Värld", close to Näs.

The Näs red house has been miraculously preserved – today it still belongs to the writer's heirs.

Das rote Haus in Näs wurde glücklicherweise erhalten und gehört heute der Familie der Schriftstellerin.

La maison rouge de Näs a été miraculeusement conservée et appartient aujourd'hui à la famille de l'écrivain.

Wenige Schriftsteller haben es geschafft, den Zauber der Kindheit so einzufangen wie Astrid Lindgren. Geboren 1907 in Näs, einem Vorort von Vimmerby in der Provinz Småland, wuchs sie auf dem Bauernhof ihrer Eltern auf, einem bescheidenen Bau, der mit dem traditionellen Ochsenblut getüncht war. Hier, in der Küche mit den rot karierten Vorhängen, unter der Petroleumlampe, ereignete sich das Wunder: Die kleine Astrid berauschte sich an den Märchen, die ihr Edit, die Tochter eines Landarbeiters, erzählte, und entdeckte die Poesie und Literatur. Später in Stockholm erfand Lindgren ihrerseits Geschichten für ihre Tochter Karin, und indem sie die Figuren Pippi Langstrumpf, Michel, Madita, Karlsson und Ronja zu Papier brachte, fand sie das verlorene Paradies ihrer Kindheit wieder. Ein Paradies, das merkwürdige Ähnlichkeit mit dem Haus in Näs hat, wo die Kinder spielten und Astrids Eltern das Ihre zur Persönlichkeitsentfaltung ihrer Kinder taten. Diese imaginäre Welt können die Fans seit 1998, einen Katzensprung von Näs entfernt, in der »Astrid Lindgrens Värld« besichtigen.

Peu d'écrivains ont su capter la magie de l'enfance comme Astrid Lindgren. Née en 1907 à Näs, un faubourg de Vimmerby dans la province de Småland, Astrid a grandi dans la ferme de ses parents, une modeste bâtisse badigeonnée du rouge sang-de-bœuf traditionnel. C'est ici, dans la cuisine aux rideaux à carreaux rouges et blancs et sous la lampe à pétrole que le miracle a eu lieu: la petite Astrid s'est enivrée des contes de fées racontés par la fille d'un laboureur, Edit, et elle a découvert la poésie et la littérature. Plus tard, à Stockholm, Lindgren, à son tour, a inventé des histoires pour sa fille Karin et, en mettant sur papier les personnages de Pippi Långstrump – Fifi Brindacier –, Zozo, Madick, Karlsson et Ronya, la fille de fermiers a retrouvé le paradis perdu de son enfance. Un paradis qui ressemblait étrangement à la maison de Näs, où les enfants jouaient jusqu'à épuisement et où les parents d'Astrid contribuèrent à l'épanouissement de la personnalité de leurs enfants. Depuis 1998, les admirateurs d'Astrid peuvent côtoyer son monde imaginaire dans le «Astrid Lindgrens Värld », situé à deux pas de Näs.

LEFT: *The kitchen at Näs has been meticulously reconstructed in "Astrid Lindgrens Värld" at Vimmerby. It is not hard to imagine Astrid as a child, sitting at the table and listening spellbound to her friend Edit's tales of Bam-Bam the giant and the fairy Viribunda.*

FACING PAGE: *Everything is ready for New Year's Eve. Astrid, her parents Samuel August and Hanna, her brother Gunnar and her sisters Stina and Ingegerd will shortly come to table.*

LINKS: *Die Küche in Näs ist in »Astrid Lindgrens Värld« in Vimmerby detailgetreu nachgebaut worden. Man kann sich lebhaft vorstellen, wie die kleine Astrid am Tisch sitzt und begierig den Geschichten ihrer Freundin Edit über Bam-Bam den Riesen und die Fee Viribunda lauscht.*

RECHTE SEITE: *Alles ist für den Silvesterabend gerichtet. Gleich werden Astrid, ihre Eltern Samuel August und Hanna, ihr Bruder Gunnar und ihre Schwestern Stina und Ingegerd am Tisch Platz nehmen.*

A GAUCHE: *La cuisine de Näs a été méticuleusement reconstruite au «Astrid Lindgrens Värld» à Vimmerby. On imagine sans peine la petite Astrid, assise à la table, et écoutant avidement les histoires de sa copine Edit sur Bam-Bam le géant et la fée Viribunda.*

PAGE DE DROITE: *Tout est prêt pour le réveillon. Astrid, ses parents Samuel August et Hanna, son frère Gunnar et ses sœurs Stina et Ingegerd vont se mettre à table.*

ACKNOWLEDGEMENTS

DANKSAGUNG

REMERCIEMENTS

The task of assembling this book has been long and arduous, and in our travels to and fro across Sweden we have had many interesting adventures and encounters. Without the unconditional support of Agnes Strojengha of Zweeds Projectburo in the Netherlands, without the backup of our loyal team at Taschen, without the help and sympathy of many museum curators and guides and the kind collaboration of the Kunglige Hovstaterna who granted the permission to photograph the Haga Pavilion, we would never have been able to complete our work. Likewise, had it not been for the kindness of all those private people who opened the doors of their manors, houses and "stugas", we would never have had the courage to finish what has amounted to a photographic marathon.

Bei unserer langen Arbeit an diesem Buch hatten wir etliche Schwierigkeiten zu bewältigen und unsere Fahrten durch Schweden hielten manche Abenteuer, aber auch unerwartete Begegnungen für uns bereit. Ohne die bedingungslose Unterstützung durch Agnes Strojengha vom Zweeds Projectburo in den Niederlanden, ohne unser treues Team bei Taschen, ohne die Sympathie und Hilfe der Museumskonservatoren und -führer und ohne die freundliche Zusammenarbeit der Kunglige Hovstaterna, die uns die Genehmigung erteilte, Aufnahmen vom Pavillon in Haga zu machen, wäre dieses Buch nie entstanden. Auch hätten wir ohne den herzlichen Empfang all derer, die uns die Türen ihres Herrensitzes, ihres Hauses oder ihrer bescheidenen »stuga« öffneten, nie den Mut gefunden, diesen fotografischen Marathon fortzusetzen.

La tâche a été longue et difficile et nos voyages à travers ce pays immense et magnifique nous réservaient bien des aventures et, surtout, des rencontres inattendues. Sans le support inconditionnel d'Agnes Strojengha du Zweeds Projectburo aux Pays-Bas, sans notre fidèle équipe de chez Taschen, sans la sympathie et l'aide des conservateurs et des guides de musées et sans l'aimable collaboration de la Kunglige Hovstaterna qui nous a autorisé à prendre des images du Pavillon de Haga, ce livre n'aurait jamais vu le jour. Nos remerciements vont aussi à tous ceux qui nous ont ouvert les portes de leur manoir, de leur maison ou de leur modeste «stuga». Leur chaleureux accueil nous a donné le courage de poursuivre ce marathon de photographie.

Barbara & René Stoeltie

In Astrid Lindgren's kitchen at Näs, Småland.

In der Küche von Astrid Lindgren in Näs, Småland.

Dans la cuisine d'Astrid Lindgren à Näs, Småland.

© 2001 TASCHEN GmbH
Hohenzollernring 53, D-50672 Köln
www.taschen.com
The reproduction of all photographs from Haga Pavilion was authorised by The Royal Court of Sweden.

Design by Catinka Keul, Cologne
Layout by Angelika Taschen, Cologne
Texts edited by Susanne Klinkhamels, Cologne
Lithography by Horst Neuzner, Cologne
English translation by Anthony Roberts, Lupiac
German translation by Stefan Barmann, Cologne

Printed in Italy
ISBN 3-8228-5702-5 (edition with German cover)
ISBN 3-8228-5868-4 (edition with English cover)
ISBN 3-8228-5734-3 (edition with French cover)